DARRYL DAVIS

How to Make $100,000+ Your First Year as a Real Estate Agent

McGraw-Hill

New York Chicago San Francisco Lisbon
London Madrid Mexico City Milan New Delhi
San Juan Seoul Singapore Toronto

The McGraw·Hill Companies

1 2 3 4 5 6 7 8 9 0 FGR/FGR 0 9 8 7

ISBN-13: 978-0-07-143759-2
ISBN-10:   0-07-143759-2

McGraw-Hill books are available at special quantity discounts to use as premiums and sales promotions, or for use in corporate training programs. For more information, please write to the Director of Special Sales, Professional Publishing, McGraw-Hill, Two Penn Plaza, New York, NY 10121-2298. Or contact your local bookstore.

Realtor® is a registered trademark of The National Association of Realtors.

This book is printed on acid-free paper.

Library of Congress Cataloging-in-Publication Data
Davis, Darryl (Darryl D.)
    How to make $100,000+ your first year as a real estate agent/ by Darryl Davis.
        p. cm.
    ISBN 0-07-143759-2 (alk. paper)
    1. Real estate business. 2. Real estate agents. I. Title II. Title: How to make one hundred thousand dollar plus your first yeat as a real estate agent.
HD1375. D326 2007
333.33023' 73—dc22   2006028080

Contents

Acknowledgments   v

Introduction   vii

1. What It Takes to Succeed as a Real Estate Agent   1

2. Getting Started   19

3. Real Estate Companies: Who's Who and What's What   35

4. Choosing the Right Company, with the Right Training, for You   49

5. Getting Organized   64

6. Prospecting: The Keys to the Kingdom   80

7. Prospecting For Sale By Owners: Dialogues and Communications That Work   99

8. Alternatives for Listing Leads Other Than For Sale By Owners: Techniques and Dialogues That Work   117

9. The Listing Conversation   147

10. Your First 90 Days of Success   171

Index   177

Acknowledgments

First and foremost, I would like to thank all the students I have trained since 1993. They have not only been an inspiration for me, but through their trial and tribulations, they have helped me to better understand the real estate industry from a training standpoint.

To the people at McGraw-Hill who have worked on this project. Their support and understanding have been incredible; I couldn't ask for a better team.

To all those in my office, for they are the backbone of my company. They help free up my time so that I can work on new programs that will help others.

To Rob Daniel, my business associate, my second spiritual guide, my pseudocoach, and, more importantly, my friend.

To Darlene Lyons, who has been such an important person in my life over these past several years. Thanks for helping me become a better speaker and a better businessman and for being my spiritual advisor.

To Uncle Jack and Aunt Nancy, who have always supported me in everything I have done and who continue to support me in everything I do. I know that no matter what, you both love me, and that gives me so much energy and life. You have always believed in me, even when I start to doubt myself. Jack, thanks for stepping in and being my role model, filling the void of Moe, and for being my consigliere.

To my son, Michael, for becoming such a wonderful young man—you are truly a gift from God, and I love you with all my heart.

Last, but most certainly not least, to Erica. I know I've said it so many times, but you are the angel in my life, and I love you for all the support you have given me and for the patience you have shown me.

Introduction

L et me congratulate you for investing in this book, *How to Make $100,000+ Your First Year as a Real Estate Agent*. More than likely, you fall into one of three categories:

- You haven't yet gotten into real estate. You're thinking about it and you are wondering, "Is this a good career for me"?
- You just got your license and you have no clue what you are doing or what you need to do. That's why you bought this book.
- You've been in real estate for some time but you aren't yet making a six-figure income, and you want to.

Wherever you are in your real estate career, I want to acknowledge you for making this investment.

There's an old rule of thumb in training that says if you speak or teach to the lowest denominator, meaning the most inexperienced person in your audience, then everybody should benefit. With that in mind, to achieve the best possible result for all readers, I'm going to communicate with you and cover the basics as if you were unlicensed and unfamiliar with the intricacies of real estate. For those of you who don't fall into that category, please hang in there with me. I promise you'll benefit as well.

So in the following pages, I will go over how to get your license, how to find to find a real estate office, questions to ask when you're on the interview, and many other things. Then, I'll give you specific tips and techniques for what you need to do to become a success in real estate.

"Success" is a relative term. And the title *How to Make $100,000+ Your First Year as a Real Estate Agent* is really representative of your market. Depending on where you're from, making a $50,000 income could be equivalent to somebody in New York who's making $100,000. However, my commitment is to get you to those six figures, and that's where I'm coming from.

Before we get started, let me offer you some tips to maximize the value of this book. First, buy yourself a spiral-bound notebook and create your own to-do list as you read. When things that I say jump out at you, jot them down. You never know when you'll be inspired!

The second tip I'll offer is, if you haven't already done so, to purchase my first book, *How to Become a Power Agent in Real Estate* (McGraw-Hill). For those of you who have read it, it has a tremendous amount of information to get you to the next level in your career.

Finally, I encourage you to go to a special Web site I designed for you, www.NewAgentSuccess.com. At that Web site, you will find a plethora of items to help you have a successful real estate career.

Many of my students have earned over $100,000 in their first year. If you follow what I share with you in this book and implement my recommendations, you can make a six-figure income your first year as well. But it's up to you.

And that's going to bring us to our first chapter. Is real estate for you? Do you have what it takes to succeed in this business?.

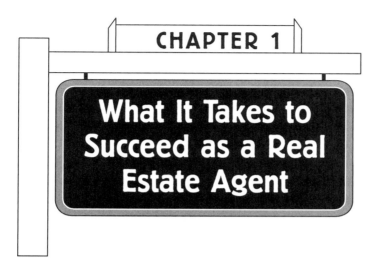

CHAPTER 1

What It Takes to Succeed as a Real Estate Agent

So, you want to be a real estate agent? I commend you for your interest in one of the most rewarding professions you can possibly choose. Of course, I'm biased, because I love what I do, and I cherish my years in this field. But, honestly, real estate is a fantastic business to enter—and not just because you can make your own hours and be extremely successful financially.

Real estate also gives you an incredible opportunity to help people with one of the most emotional and intensely rewarding experiences they can have: the purchase or sale of their own home.

In this chapter, you'll get a brief background on the skills and personal characteristics you need to succeed in real estate. You will also learn about the economic basics of real estate—how you make your money and the steps you need to take to be financially fit. And, finally, you'll find out how to make certain that your family is on board for what can sometimes be a bumpy ride as you begin your new career.

It Takes Commitment

Many would-be agents don't see all the hard work that successful agents have to put in to get where they are. After all, it's pretty easy to get licensed to sell real estate. Many people who enter the field are looking for part-time employment or a second job. There's nothing wrong with motivations such as these. Yet, many people with a part-time attitude don't have the commitment necessary to succeed. Real estate is not a hobby, it's a business. You can't "dabble" in it and achieve great results. That's why many beginners soon drop out.

This is a 100 percent commission field, and if you don't produce, you don't earn. But you can prepare yourself to enter this profession and best ensure your success, which you'll find out about shortly.

First, let's explore *your* possible motivations for entering the field of real estate. People get into real estate for a lot of different reasons. Perhaps you have been part of a downsizing and you need to reinvent yourself. Maybe you're going through a divorce and you've got to take care of yourself financially. It could be that you're a young person looking for a career that you can start quickly and enjoy and also make decent money right away. Or, real estate might be a stepping-stone to something else that you want to do in your life; it's the tool or the vehicle to help get you to that next level.

Whatever scenario is true for you, you can make over a six-figure income in real estate. But it does depend on you. First, you need to look at yourself as a person and figure out your overall outlook on life.

Your attitude is more important than anything else you have for determining how successful you will be in the field. A good way to think about attitude is to think of it as your "context." For example, there's a key difference between *content* and *context*. If you had a glass, the glass would be the context that would hold the water, which is the content. The context, the glass, gives shape to the content, the water. The water—the content—is great, but it is completely useless to drink unless you have a glass—the context. So if I gave you the content—effective listing and selling techniques to make six figures your first year in real estate—but the context of who you are as a person, your attitude and outlook, is not that of a can-do self-starter but instead that of a complainer and a whiner, then no matter what I do, all the tools and success strategies in the world are not going to help. Your positive attitude is the "glass" that holds the success strategies. Without the glass, the water has no place to go. So, the chance of your becoming a true success your first year in real estate is totally up to you.

Here's how I approached the field of real estate: I got into it as a stepping-stone. It didn't end up that way, but that's how it began. My dad passed away when I was 14, and my mom wasn't able to deal with it. So it fell on my shoulders to bury my dad—pick out the casket and make the arrangements for the funeral. I also had to get my own apartment at 16, while still in high school, and had to support myself. I worked at many places, as a clerk at a local supermarket, as a security guard at a high-end condominium, and on the weekends at a nightclub. (I lied about my age; that was before I learned how important integrity was.)

So, in my teenage years, I went through some very hard knocks in my personal life. You, too, may be going through personal difficulties. Learn from me that you can overcome obstacles that come your way.

At 19, I went to college and I majored in theater arts. But with acting, you're either rich and famous or you're broke and struggling. So I decided to get into real estate because somebody told me it was a great profession. I could make my own hours (we'll talk about that bogus supposition later!) and still pursue my acting career. Real estate consumed me—in a good way. I did really well, averaging six transactions a month, so I phased out of acting. And I truly love what I'm doing now.

Enough about me; let's turn the spotlight on you. Here are the personal traits you need to possess to make it big in real estate.

Characteristics of Top Agents

Characteristic 1: Be Committed to Education

Obviously, you are already committed to education, otherwise you would not have purchased this book. But don't ever stop. In my experience traveling all over the United States, Canada, New Zealand, and Australia training agents agents on how to increase their production, there's one common denominator that I've noticed in agents who make over six figures: They're always in some kind of training program. They're always taking some kind of course or seminar, or they're getting personal coaching from experts. They're investing in themselves, consistently improving personally, because they realize that *they* are the most important product in their real estate business.

A lot of new agents come into the business very excited. "I'm a sponge," they say, "give it to me. I can absorb it. I can learn it. I'll do anything!" They're almost like children who want to learn everything. "Mommy, Daddy, how does this work?" And then, all of a sudden, they become teenagers. And now, the learning stops. Now, they know it all. It's "I know, I know. Leave me alone." Well, unfortunately, that describes 80 percent of experienced agents.

In my view, four out of five experienced agents believe that they already know all they need to know about how to do their job. And they're the ones struggling to get to the next level in real estate. But the ones who are making six-figure incomes and more don't think like this. They're always in some kind of coaching or training program, they're going to conferences, and they're listening to audio CDs. Most of the new agents I've worked with also share this attitude. But, like children who are naturally inquisitive when they *start* learning, after a while they become "teenagers" who think they have all the answers and want to be left alone.

So, I hope that you keep your open-mindedness. Keep seeing the world (and, in particular, your profession) through a child's eye. Like the top agents in the world, keep looking at how you can learn more and get to the next level in your career.

Characteristic 2: Focus on Vision

In my live seminars, I sometimes ask the audience, "What do you think is the most important piece to a jigsaw puzzle?" The answers are always different: the last piece, the centerpiece, or even the corners. The truth is, the most important piece is the box cover. Why? Because that is where the picture is showing you what the final result should look like. In order for you to be truly successful, you need to have a vision, a picture, of how you want your career to look.

The majority of agents come into this business all excited, all hyped up, all turned on. "Yes, I'm going into real estate. I'm going to get my license, and I'm going to make a ton of money!" This is their initial vision. But all of a sudden, doors start closing in their faces, people selling their property themselves (the "For Sale By Owners") are hanging up on them, deals are falling through, and before you know it, these agents are on antidepressants. It can be real easy for you to get emotionally drained and depressed.

In his book, *Seven Habits of Highly Effective People*, acclaimed author Steven Covey says that you and I have an emotional bank account. Other people make either deposits or withdrawals from this account. And it's easy, in this business, for people to take withdrawals from us. So you need to put things into perspective to help you replenish yourself and remember why you're doing this.

Every successful person, whether a musician, an artist, an Olympian, or an investment banker, went through some sort of pain, be it emotional, mental, or physical. You're also going to go through some pain to be a top agent. And what's going to make you successful is your ability to push past the pain. Agents who are ordinary stop when they feel pain. They get paralyzed, they go home, they put on a robe, and they eat popcorn and watch TV. So what's going to push you past your pain? You've got to have a vision that's bigger than who you are now.

First, get out of debt, no matter what kind. One of the things that can hold you back from being really great in real estate is the stress of money. Or, better said, the stress of *lack* of money. If you're always chasing the dollar, coming from an attitude of scarcity, you won't succeed. Whatever you're focused on most, that's what the universe gives you. So, if you're focused on not having enough money, you're going to stay that way. But when you are debt-free, you're liberated. You can play. You can think about your next level.

Next, when you focus on real estate be sure that it's what you *want* to focus on. That, too, can prevent you from fulfilling your career dream. For example, back in the days when I did one-on-one coaching with agents, one student was really doing poorly. I said to her, "If you could have anything in your life and you could be doing anything, what would it be?" And she said, "Honestly? I'd like to be a teacher."

Now, most teachers, as you know, don't make top dollar. But she just loved working with children. So we determined what she needed to do to become a teacher. After that, she had a breakthrough in her career. She kicked butt. Within a year, she had the money she needed to go back to school and finish her studies to become a teacher. And that's just what she did. She got out of real estate. It was what *she* was committed to.

Be clear about what *your* vision is. It might be something material that you want to obtain, or a lifestyle (like living debt-free) that you want to achieve. Once you're clear about precisely what it is, I want you to create what I call a Vision Board. A Vision Board, quite simply, is a posterboard filled with pictures, words, and phrases that represent your vision. It may sound somewhat like a high school or even a grammar school project, but it works. Go to the bookstore and get magazines that depict the life you want to lead, whether it involves luxury items or neighborhoods or family goals. Start cutting out either pictures or words that represent your vision. No matter what happens, this is the reason that you're in real estate. Look at your board at least once a day and stay focused on your vision.

Characteristic 3: Set a High CAP

CAP is an acronym that stands for Confidence, Aggressiveness, and Persistence. How much money you make in real estate will be greatly influenced by how strong these three personality traits are for you. Let me go over each of these.

Confidence

When the most successful agents go on listing appointments and they're talking to sellers about hiring them, they're coming in with an air of confidence. You, too, need this. For example, suppose you want to get listings, one of the hardest things to obtain in our business. You've got to go to homeowners and sell yourself. You've got to convince them that you are the best, wisest choice. If you're not confident in yourself, if you don't believe that the homeowners should hire you rather than somebody else, if *you're* not sold on yourself, then how can *they* be sold on you? Just think, if you were going to hire a professional such as a doctor or lawyer, wouldn't you want someone who walked that fine line between confidence and arrogance?

So your next question should be: how can I become more confident? The answer is simple: the more knowledge you have, the more confident you become. If you go on a listing appointment knowing everything there is to know about the business, certainly more than the homeowner knows, that gives you an edge, and you'll feel more secure. So, invest the time, energy, and (sometimes) expense necessary to become more knowledgeable. Go through training courses. Get personal coaching. Talk to other experienced agents. Visit www.NewAgentSuccess.com and find out about one of my live events.

Know this: getting your real estate license is your admission to the University of Hard Knocks. But, unfortunately, in almost every state in the United States or province in Canada, the education that you receive to get your license is typically more involved with the legal side of real estate (contracts, liability, and so on). They don't teach you listing and selling skills. That's where seminars and the information in this book come in handy. I can't stress it enough. You need to continuously improve your education. It's a crucial step to your success.

Aggressiveness

Don't mistake pushiness, obnoxiousness, or violent behavior for aggressiveness. Being aggressive means having to go out and get the business. You have to truly believe, which I hope you will by the end of this book, that homeowners should *never* sell their houses on their own. If they're doing that, they're making a huge mistake, costing themselves significant money and time. If selling a house were as simple as putting an ad in the paper, you wouldn't have to be licensed by your state to help other people do it, right? Selling a house takes knowledge, skill, and ability. So, when you're on listing appointments talking to homeowners about hiring you, you need to be confident and somewhat aggressive, because you know it's in their best interest to hire you.

Note: it's not in *your* best interest, but in *theirs*. The focus is on serving other people. When it is, success will follow. As I tell my son and my students, money is merely a gauge as to how many people we've helped in our lives. This is true regardless of your profession. As a professional real estate agent, the more people you help, the more money you make! So we need to be aggressive in helping people, for their own good.

Another area in which you also need to be aggressive is prospecting. You've got to go out and get the business. You can't wait for it to come to you; you've got to go out and get it. Agents who are making six figures are not sitting in their offices waiting for the phone to ring. As a matter of fact, you hardly ever see them in their offices because they are either out on appointments, knocking on doors, or showing property. You don't make money sitting in the real estate office. You've got to go out and get it.

Persistence

You need to be able to handle rejection. People will say "no" to you; they will hang up on you; they even may not like you. How to handle that? Great agents are like Super Balls. They bounce back really high. If you take a Super Ball and you hold it at chest level and drop it, that ball will usually bounce up past where you let go of it. Now, that's what I mean by persistence! That when you fall down, you will actually bounce back higher than where you started.

Consider the story of my son, Michael. When he was five, I taught him how to play checkers, and we've been playing ever since. My game-playing style with my son is to always play full out, to never just let him win. I figured if I were really tough on him as a little boy it would make him stronger as an adult. But when Michael would lose, he would get so upset. He sometimes would take the board and throw it. He actually started to do this *before* he would lose if he knew that he was on his way to losing. I would always say to him, "Michael, losing is not a bad thing." Because, I'm thinking that if this is how he is at five years of age with checkers, when he starts playing the real game of life, it's going to be worse for him.

So, I'm trying to train my son on how to embrace failure; how to embrace mistakes. Warren Buffett said in his autobiography that success is the worst teacher because you only learn from your failures. So I keep telling my son, "Michael, mistakes are good because you learn from them." It came to the point where checkers was just a vehicle for me to teach my son the concept of breakdowns enabling breakthroughs. If you don't experience a problem, you can't grow from figuring out the solution. Nietzsche said that "that which does not kill us makes us stronger." I believe that's true.

Interestingly, about four months into this exercise of teaching checkers to my son, sure enough he wins! And I just couldn't believe a five-year-old boy could beat me at checkers. When I lost this game, I looked at him, stunned, and said, "I can't believe that just happened!" And what does Michael say to me? "Daddy, that's okay because you learn from your mistakes!" Well, thank goodness he got my point.

What can you take from this story? Just this: a lot of agents simply don't succeed because they are afraid of losing and they don't give themselves permission to make mistakes. They want to do it "the right way" the very first time they try something. So, until they master the business and all of the dialogues and scripts and techniques, they're not going to even try. They practice, practice, practice. But when it comes time to actually picking up the phone and calling a For Sale By Owner, they won't because they still don't feel they're ready. They can't handle even the thought of rejection or failure. So, remember: every time you make a mistake, you learn from it and you become stronger, and that comes from being persistent.

If you excel at Confidence, Aggressiveness, and Persistence, your CAP value will be high, and so will your income!

Characteristic 4: Have a Business Owner Mentality

Top agents don't look at themselves as salespeople. They view themselves as businesspeople. Some agents don't learn this until they're well into their real estate careers. By telling you this now, I'm taking *years* off your learning curve!

Let's say you're going to open up a pizzeria. What would you have to do? What items would you have to start taking care of? You would have to come up with a plan, right? For finding a store location. For the décor. For hiring people. For the products you'll need to purchase. For the money you'll need to raise. Clearly, it's not just about sales. It's a full-fledged business. Whether it's a pizza store or a hair salon, there are numerous business items you must tackle.

The same is true about real estate. If you do that, right out of the gate, you will be way ahead of other agents. To be a good businessperson, you must excel in a number of areas, which we'll explore in greater detail later in this book. These areas include money management, utilization of technology, organizational skills, communication skills, direct mail advertising, print advertising, and customer service.

Characteristic 5: Be a Problem Solver

To be an effective owner, you must master the ability to go with the flow. In his book, *In Search of Excellence*, Tom Peters, a brilliant corporate management guru who became very popular in the later 1980s and early 1990s, said, "You cannot manage chaos, because the more you try and manage it, the more the chaos manages you." Real estate can be very chaotic: there are deals falling apart, basements leaking, multiple timetables to manage, funding coming undone, poor inspection reports, and so on. You need to be able to have it all roll off your back. Then, you need to roll up your sleeves, get creative, and solve problems.

A good friend of mine, Steve Harney, once told me, "Real estate is not a science where two plus two equals four. It's more of an art." So, be creative, go with the flow, and find a way to accomplish what needs to be done.

Keep in mind, as you read this book, that you might not understand everything, and it might even drive you a little crazy. But every new agent I've ever met has gone through that feeling of being overwhelmed and confused in the beginning. Don't worry. You don't need to understand it all right now; eventually you will. There is an old saying: when the student is ready, the teacher will appear. You will understand it all when you are ready to understand it.

A word of caution as you start your new career: be cautious of advice from other agents in your office. My experience has taught me that agents who are not doing well are usually the ones who are quick to give you their opinion. That is so because it's human nature to justify, when a particular venture is not going well, that that's just the way things are; it's *other* people's fault, and it has nothing to do with one's own culpability. In other words, misery loves company. It's easier for an agent to blame the broker, the economy, the politicians—whomever—than to take personal responsibility for how his or her career looks. So when a new agent comes into the office and starts kicking butt by making a six-figure income, that forces the agent who's been there for five years and is struggling financially to reexamine the situation. The new agent can do it, so why not the long-timer? To make him- or herself look better, the long-timer just might want to offer advice to the new kid on the block. And how good can that be? So you want to be careful with the agent who is quick to offer pearls of wisdom about your office or your market.

You'll want to make friends and build relationships in your office, and that goal is important. But be careful that you don't get involved in a "he said, she said" type of conversation about other people behind their backs. Sometimes you think you're getting *educated* from behind the scenes, but actually you're getting *sucked into* something. Hang around the positive, productive people. There's a rule of thumb saying that your income is the average of that of your five closest friends. If that's true, make sure your five closest friends in real estate are the most financially productive effective people you can find.

Bear in mind that the productive agents are usually the last ones to give you advice. That's so for two reasons. Number one, they are usually too busy to worry about somebody else. It's not that they don't care about the other agents in their offices, but their focus is on taking care of themselves, their families, and their clients. Reason number two, which is the more common one, is that the top agents don't know how to transfer the knowledge of what they do that works so well for them to someone else. They never even really stopped to think about what they do. They're like a Tiger Woods: they just do. Actually they don't just do, they just "are." It's second nature to them because they've gotten to that level in their careers where they do without thinking anymore. Stay tough. The first year is going to be your hardest year. But if you hang in there that first year, eventually you will break the six-figure barrier, especially if you follow the guidelines established in this book.

Where Does the Time Go?

Let's now examine the basics of the job of real estate agent. Later on we'll come back to the individual aspects of the job, which will be discussed in more detail.

The most important part of the job, which I estimate to take up at least 40 percent of your time, is going to be prospecting. Prospecting can take many different forms. The most popular is making phone calls. There are different types of phone calls. One is calling homeowners who are trying to sell their properties on their own. Another is calling people who tried working with an agent on a Multiple Listing Service and who have had the listing expire. Still another is your friends, family, and sphere of influence. You've got to tap into those people or at least let them know that you're in real estate. In addition to using the telephone, you should knock on doors, network with other business owners, and do self-promotion. So there are a number of ways to generate business and prospects.

Much of your time and your energy—about 25 percent, I estimate—will be working with buyers. That means inspecting and showing property, qualifying them, and even putting together real estate transactions. Another 25 percent of your time will be taken up servicing sellers, advertising, communicating with sellers, doing open houses, and the like. The last 10 percent of your time will be spent doing the miscellaneous stuff: attending office meetings, sending e-mails, doing paperwork, and so on.

So, what should you glean from this general overview? Let me reiterate, as this point is very important: *prospecting is the most important point of the job.*

Consider this story about a conversation I had recently. One of my students is a middle-aged gentleman who has a family that counts on him financially. We were having this great conversation about his business. He said, "Dale, I'm not doing well this year." The bottom line is that he's not making a lot of money. So I said, "Look, it's very simple. Number one is, we make money in real estate in two areas. That's working with sellers and working with buyers. You can model your business on working with buyers—showing property, qualifying them, taking them out. But you can't force somebody to buy a home."

Correct? If that's your business model, you're going to focus your energy in showing houses and working with buyers. You've got a 50-50 shot there if you're going to make money, and if you want to make it quickly.

But the drawback in working with buyers and having that be your business model is that it can drain the heck out of you.

This particular agent I was talking to said: "Yeah, I don't want to do that. I've been working with three buyers, and all three bought houses through me. I was pretty excited about it, and all of a sudden all three of the buyers changed their minds after the home inspections came back just a little negative. They got cold feet and backed out of the contracts."

Here's this agent who's struggling. This agent has a wife and children to support. He had counted on this money from these three contracts, and they fell through. And it took about a month for him to find this out. So, there are 30 days of being happy and then, all of a sudden, crashing. Buyers can really put you through an emotional roller coaster. Do you want to base your business model on them?

On the other hand, if you're working with sellers and you have homeowners who have hired you to sell their homes and you build your business based on that, you've got a much more solid business model. So, once again, if you really want to be successful and make a six-figure income in real estate, at least 40 percent of your energy has to be in just prospecting for listings. Quite frankly, if you were a smart businessperson, you would focus 100 percent of your energy on just getting listings; then, after your sixth one, you would start showing properties to buyers.

Working with Sellers versus Working with Buyers

Let's examine advantages and disadvantages of working with buyers and sellers. As you know, I think that working with sellers is the way to go. But what follows will give you a balanced view of both.

Advantages of Working with Sellers

One of the major advantages of working with sellers is that there's a certain level of commitment when they sign a listing with you; in essence, they say, "Here's my house, and I'm committing to selling it." With buyers, even if they commit to buying a house through you (and there's a document they could sign called the *buyer-agency agreement*), you still cannot force them to buy the house. Of course, with sellers, if they change their minds, it's the same thing. But the bottom line is there's a level of commitment with sellers that you don't see with buyers.

Another advantage to working with sellers is that you can be on vacation and still make money. Let's say, hypothetically, you have 10 listings—10 homeowners who have hired you. You've put their houses on the market through the Multiple Listing Service. Other agents are showing the properties. They can be showing the properties to other buyers while you're in Hawaii, sitting on the beach and drinking a margarita.

Another advantage to working with sellers is that you're more in control of the transaction when you are on the listing side of the contract. The sellers dictate the terms to the buyers. Here's what they want. Here's the price. Here are the terms. Here's the closing date. So the sellers are in the driver's seat. When you have sellers and you have buyers and you're negotiating an offer, if that offer doesn't get accepted, doesn't get put together, or falls apart, whatever the case may be, you still have the listing. Buyers, on the other hand, can change their minds, work with another agent, or decide not to buy at all because they are discouraged.

The major advantage to working with sellers is that when you're working only the buyer side of the transaction, the most you can ever make is just that one side of the transaction. But if you are a listing agent *and* you have the listing, you can make the listing side of the transaction and, if you happen to show your property yourself, you'll have the buyer's side of the transaction too. You'll make double the money on one transaction. When you work with buyers, you don't have that opportunity.

Disadvantages of Working with Sellers

There are disadvantages with working with sellers, too. The first disadvantage is that you need to generate appointments. You need to be somewhat aggressive in generating those listing appointments, finding sellers, and having conversations with them. Also, sellers who are trying to sell on their own do not want to work with agents, unlike buyers who want to work with agents most of the time. So, you've got to convince the sellers why they should work with agents and that you are the best person to work for them. It takes money to promote yourself to generate listings, and it takes money to service the listings once you get them, to get those properties sold.

Advantages of Working with Buyers

What are the advantages of working with buyers? The main one is that is that it's relatively easy. You take buyers out. You show them a house. You don't need a lot of skill or technique to do that, so it's less stressful. In addition, you're working with people who want to work with you, and that makes the process more enjoyable. Also, buyers can become your future sellers.

Disadvantages of Working with Buyers

The disadvantage to working with buyers is that you get only one side of the transaction. You're not in control of the sales process. You can't force these people to buy, and in many cases it takes more time to make a lot of money when you work with buyers. There is one other disadvantage too. Buyers can drain you emotionally. You can be showing buyers house after house, weekend after weekend. You can be working with buyers for 60 or 90 days and still not have anything come together. Worse, you can be working with buyers, write a contract, and then suddenly the deal falls apart for any one of a multitude of reasons, and now you're emotionally drained from the experience.

Commercial Real Estate

How Commercial Real Estate Differs from Residential Real Estate

Commercial real estate deals primarily with the leasing or selling of commercial buildings and/or businesses. Residential real estate, of course, deals primarily with private residences.

Let me outline some of the advantages and disadvantages of this area of real estate.

Advantages of Commercial Real Estate

Very professional atmosphere. Dealing with commercial real estate prospects is very different from dealing with the average person who is looking to buy or sell the family home. When you are working with buyers/lessees (the *lessee* is the person who rents from the owner/landlord) or sellers/lessors (the *lessor* is the owner of the property that is renting to the tenant) who own, want to own, or want to rent buildings that are worth millions of dollars, you are attracting a very sophisticated type of individual. Naturally, the type of salesperson that works best with these individuals has a similarly sophisticated way about her- or himself. In addition, the money that is spent on staff, technology, furnishings, and so on, is all geared toward that sophisticated type of clientele.

More money per sale. Because of the price of the commercial properties, you can make tens of thousands of dollars from just one lease or sale. You don't have to sell a lot of commercial properties to make a six-figure income.

Normal business hours. Traditionally, commercial agents work a nine-to-five schedule because their clientele works that type of schedule. This certainly gives you the opportunity to easily balance your family life with your business life.

Suitable style for you. If you enjoy being analytical and working in a Fortune 500 type of atmosphere, then working with commercial real estate could be a very good choice for you. But, as in any sales profession, you still need to be aggressive in prospecting to generate your own business. Just as with residential real estate, the firm will not just hand you business; you have to go out and get it.

Disadvantages of Commercial Real Estate

Very competitive. The expression "only the strong survive" is true in residential real estate, but it is particularly so in commercial real estate. Agents are looking to land the "big fish" so that they can make the big sale with the big commission check. You have to definitely have that competitive instinct to survive.

Securing a deal is time consuming. It is not uncommon for it to take one to two years to generate just one commercial transaction. So, unless you have enough money saved or enough cash flow from another source to pay your personal bills for at least a year, you should not venture into commercial real estate.

A great deal of knowledge is needed. Commercial real estate is a specialty, which requires a great deal of skill and knowledge. You will need to be able to do the following:

- Evaluate mortgage loans using compounding and discounting techniques
- Calculate amortization values
- Apply compounding and discounting techniques to investment decisions
- Calculate internal rate of return for a variety of different investment scenarios

- Know the tax issues that affect the acquisition, operation, and disposition of commercial real estate investments
- Know the benefits and drawbacks of the sale leaseback transaction for users and sellers and investors
- Quantify the net present value (NPV) of continuing to own and occupy a property for a specific period of time versus the net present value of the cash flows associated with selling and leasing back that property for the same period of time

The Commercial Agent Test

The following are a few questions to ask in order to determine whether or not being a commercial agent is for you.

Are you a risk taker? Commercial real estate is about taking risks and gambles, about trying all different angles (legal, of course) to put together a deal. Sometimes your gambles work, and sometimes they backfire. If you tend to be somewhat conservative and traditional, then residential real estate is the place for you.

Do you need to work in a corporate environment? New agents who come from corporate America sometimes get frustrated by how noncorporate the residential real estate industry in the United States is. Agents make their own hours, plodding along trying to make their careers work. If you like the corporate feeling, if you need the structure provided by a nine-to-five job, then commercial real estate may be more fitting for you.

Are you more analytical or are you more emotional? The word *emotional* here doesn't mean that you are an emotional basket case. Unlike commercial clients, residential customers base most of their buying and selling decisions on emotions and feelings. If you prefer dealing with facts and figures, then commercial real estate would be more suited to your style.

When you become licensed by your state to practice real estate, you can work in both commercial and residential real estate. My experience is that it is best to pick one or the other. Agents who try to do both rarely succeed (they are a "jack of all trades" but master of none). Of course, as with anything, there is always the exception to the rule. You can find agents who are successful at doing both (some recent students come to mind), but my advice is to focus on only one area. If you decide to pursue commercial real estate, there are plenty of books that can help you on the topic. For recommended readings and commercial organizations, go to my Web site: www.NewAgentSuccess.com.

Investing in Real Estate

One of the most overlooked opportunities for real estate agents is investing in real estate. Although this book is not about this wonderful area of creating wealth, I would be remiss if I didn't write a word or two about it.

As a real estate agent, you are in the best position to find real estate investment opportunities. You see properties and know about properties that are coming up for sale before the general public is aware of them. This gives you a huge advantage. Let me show you how if you were to buy just one investment property, you could set yourself up for retirement. Let's say you buy a house for $300,000 and rent it out so that the rent pays all the expenses of ownership, and let's say there is no profit; in other words, the house pays for itself. Let's also assume that the house, on the average, appreciates 5 percent a year (some years will be less, and some will be more). When you add the appreciation of the house, plus the paying down of the mortgage principal, after 15 years you would have amassed $393,332.29 of profit. This doesn't even include the tax benefits you would have received. Now, if you had three properties like this, you would be worth over $1 million in 15 years. This is not make-believe; these are actual numbers.

For example, when I started in real estate 20 years ago, I struck up a friendship with a man named Mac Levitt, who was also starting out. He bought real estate investments regularly during the next 20 years. Now, Mac has amassed a small fortune in real estate, along with owning four real estate offices. Be like Mac; spend time looking for investment opportunities while you are working in real estate. Set a goal to buy just one house a year. If you do that, you will probably be worth millions in 15 years.

It's time to find out how to get started in real estate. Turn to Chapter 2 for some good pointers.

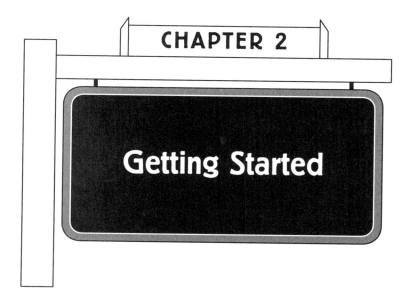

CHAPTER 2

Getting Started

What things do you need to do to get underway in your business? Here you'll first find out about the money you need to have and to spend in order to survive in your business and your personal life. Then, you'll learn about the arrangements you need to make with your family and yourself to allow some balance between your business and personal lives.

What Does It Cost to Get Started?

For you to survive in this business, you've got to have two things. You've got to have personal money in order to take care of yourself and your family during the lean times. Then you've got to have money so that your real estate business doesn't go under when things get tough. Let's start with the personal.

Personal Expenses

With the personal, what you need to do is figure out what it costs you to survive each month—in other words, how much are your essential bills. Add up all your expenses for the month for the following items:

- Mortgage payment
- Credit card payments
- Car payment
- School loans
- Anything else that is a regular monthly bill, such as food, dry-cleaning, gas, and utilities

Now you simply multiply your total monthly personal bills by 12 months and you will know what you need to survive on a yearly basis.

There are other personal costs to consider as well, like retirement planning and financial planning. For more information and a plethora of support material about this, go to www.NewAgent Success.com.

Business Expenses

The next number for you to determine is your business expenses. The number will be different for each person, because every market is different. So figuring out how much you need to run your real estate business is up to you. This area is one in which your broker or manager can be very helpful. What I recommend is that you go to www.New AgentSuccess.com, print out the spreadsheet of business expenses, sit down with your broker-manager, and have him or her help you determine the actual costs of each item on that sheet. In the meantime, the following are some items you need to consider:

Realtor Association and Multiple Listing Service dues. When you join and work with a broker who is part of the National Association of Realtors, you will need to pay some dues: national dues, state dues, and dues for the local Board of Realtors. In addition, there are the Multiple Listing Service dues. The Multiple Listing Service is one of the biggest tools that agents use to help sellers get their houses sold. It's basically a network of all the brokers on a local and national level. So when one agent lists a house for sale, he or she puts it into the computer system, the Multiple Listing Service (MLS for short). Then all the agents in the market and throughout the nation can get access to that housing information. We will go over this great tool in more detail in Chapter 5.

Insurance. As an independent contractor, you must carry Errors and Omission (E&O) insurance. This is an insurance policy that protects you in the event you should misrepresent something to a buyer, seller, or both. This type of insurance is similar to malpractice insurance for a doctor.

Car expenses. You are going to be driving around much more than you have in the past, so you need to budget for the extra expenses for gas and car repairs.

Education. Your education is one of the most important areas in which you will need to keep investing. One of my sayings is *the more you learn, the more you will earn*. See Chapters 4 and 6 for more of what you need to consider in terms of education (and education expenses).

Advertising. There are two kinds of advertising: large advertising and small advertising. The former consists of large amounts of monthly mailings or of ads in your major local newspaper or in the Yellow Pages. In other words, it involves things that will cost you a large amount of money. For a new agent, I don't recommend you go this route unless you can afford it. But small advertising is smart. For example, let's say you belong to a church, temple, or synagogue. Your house of worship probably has some kind of newsletter it gives to its congregation, and it probably won't charge you very much to place an ad in that newsletter. This way you would reach many people. Another example of small advertising would be placing an ad in a community newsletter.

Technology tools. Because there are so many different technology tools for an agent to invest in, the effort can become overwhelming. My advice is to start slow and do your research. Here are a few items I recommend you investigate:

- **A laptop.** A laptop computer is better than a desktop computer simply because it gives you the freedom to work wherever you want. Plus, you can bring it with you on a listing appointment. Nowadays, laptops are very inexpensive.

- **Laser printer.** Nowadays, color laser printers are very reasonably priced. I'm sure your real estate office has one you can use, but it may be a good idea to have one at home.
- **Digital camera.** This is a necessary tool for when you get your listings. Make sure the camera has the ability to take short video, say about five minutes' worth of footage. You can use this feature to get a testimonial from a happy customer; then you can upload that testimonial onto your laptop computer and play the video for a potential seller.
- **Palm Pilot.** I believe this is one of the best tools to help you stay organized. Some Multiple Listing Services in the United States give you the ability to search for listings right there on your Palm Pilot.

Office supplies. You will need to invest in little things such as business cards, stationery, pens, and the like. Your broker-manager can direct you about where to order your stationery.

Car magnets. Car magnets are not very expensive, but they give you great exposure. People can find everyday uses for them: on refrigerator doors, on office walls, on car doors, on bulletin boards, and so on. People who see the magnets naturally assume that if you are bold enough to advertise yourself that way, you will be equally bold in marketing a house for sale.

If money is not a concern, there are some optional things you can look at doing for your business, which are described below.

Optional Expenses

Web site. A Web site can generate some leads and is a great way to position yourself as being an expert in the field. Developing and operating a Web site takes time, however, and it can cost a good amount of money. Also, make sure you delegate the design of the site to someone else. If you want a Web design company, I recommend going to www.NewAgentSuccess.com for some leads.

Monthly mailings. Mailings are about *future* business. It's about positioning yourself for something that's going to happen. If you were to take 1,000 people and mail them something (a flyer, a promotional notice, a letter, or something similar) every four weeks, and if you did that for about 9 to 12 months, you would start to get leads from this group of 1,000. It is absolutely crucial that you do this consistently. In other words, you cannot miss one mailing. If you do, it's as if you started to push a boulder up a hill and just when you're about to reach the top, you decide to take a break. What happens to that boulder? It slides down, and now you have to start all over again. When you miss one of your monthly mailings, the same effect occurs. To reemphasize: do not start a mailing campaign unless you know what you're mailing out and you're prepared to go with it for at least 12 months.

Large advertising. One of the things you can do to really promote yourself and to expedite things is to ask other agents in your office if you could advertise some of their listings so that you could generate some of your own buyers. I don't recommend that you do this. Instead, you should be generating other listings. Now, why would I suggest you advertise other agents' listings? Well, it's rare that other sellers will call on those, because the people who are actually going to call are buyers. What you can do with those buyer calls is give them to other agents in your office and collect referral fees (we'll talk about this later in the book). But the whole point in advertising other agents' listings is that if you run a few of these ads, when you go on listing appointments and you're talking to sellers, you can show them the type of advertising you do. Now when they see your face and they see the houses that you're advertising, they'll naturally assume they are your listing and also that if you've got several listings, you must have been in real estate for a while. They won't ever think to ask you how long you've been doing this or think that you're new.

New car. You may want to consider buying or leasing a new car, if you can afford it and if you think you need it. It's not essential to have a brand-new car, but you don't want to have a real clinker either.

Advertising premiums. Advertising premiums are little promotional items such as pens, rulers, notepads, calendars, and the like. They do not generate business, but they are a way to promote yourself. For more on advertising, see Chapter 8.

At this point, you should have a pretty good understanding of what you need to cover your personal expenses and your business expenses. Now you need to calculate exactly how much you need to make it all work.

Calculating Exactly How Much You Need for Personal Expenses and Business Expenses

To calculate how much you will need, let's say for you just to survive you need $30,000 a year for your personal expenses. Then, let's say, based on determinations you make with your broker-manager, you need $20,000 to break even on your business expenses. So, if you add your personal expenses of $30,000 and your business expenses of $20,000, that's a total of $50,000. Now you need to put taxes on top of that (see below), and let's do, as a rule of thumb, 20 percent, which is $10,000. Your total is now $60,000.

Seems okay, right? Well, if you look at these numbers, you are basically only surviving. And you're not in real estate just to survive, are you? You want to get to the next level. So, I'd like you to determine what your vision goals are and what they cost. For example, part of your vision may be to pay off your debt. Or it may be to buy an investment piece of property or to start college funds for your kids or to buy a second car, a vacation home, or a new car. So, what's your fun money? What are all of the things that you would like to achieve? Let's say they cost $40,000. Add it all up, and it comes to $100,000.

Here's a sad reality (most brokers won't tell this to new agents): you have to assume it will take you at least six months before you start to generate any money from real estate. It could happen more quickly, but you should plan for the worst-case scenario. Based on the example we are using, if your personal expenses, business expenses, and taxes for the year total $60,000, that means you need to have at least $30,000 in savings ($60,000/2 [6 months] = $30,000).

This really needs to sink in. The first day you start your new career in real estate, you don't have any money coming in, unless of course you've got a spouse who is covering your personal expenses. If that's the case, you're very fortunate, because now you can have fun in real estate and not have stress and worries about money.

If you're one of those 80 percent who does not have someone paying your personal bills, then you may be coming into real estate with money concerns. Assuming you sold a house (and again, I don't want you to be working with buyers) in your first 60 days, it's going to be about four months until you see your first commission check. It's also possible you could have to wait for seven to nine months to see money coming in. So, you need to be prepared with six months of your expenses covered. To be really secure, it would be great to have nine months saved. That amount would give you some freedom from the stress that can plague an agent who is not well prepared.

There is another reason to have at least six months of your personal and business expenses covered. According to the Small Business Administration (SBA), the number-one reason why most businesses go out of business, especially the restaurant business (it has a very high failure rate), is that they don't have enough money to pay their bills. They don't have enough reserve money to weather the storm.

For example, say you're going to start a restaurant. What do you need to open up the business? You've got to find a location, right? You've got to repair that place or build it. You've got to put the kitchen in, and then you've got to buy the furniture. Then you need promotional money to advertise the restaurant. You've got to hire your staff and buy food. So you need all this money to get started. Now, let's say all this startup money comes to $100,000. In addition, you'll need money every week to cover overhead. Every week, you'll have to cover salary for the employees and for yourself and buy additional supplies. There are monthly expenses for rent and utilities. You will need $100,000 just to open up the doors and perhaps another $250,000 to cover all those expenses for the next year. And if you don't have at least six months of that money set up, then for the first week that you're open, you will be worried about making payroll, making rent, and paying the utilities.

Most people are so shortsighted. They just look at *here's how much money I need to open up the doors*. But you have to have money in place to carry you for those first 6 to 12 months. As a real estate agent, you need to cover the first 6 months, minimum. That's my opinion. Your broker or manager may tell you something a little bit different. But listen to me. Always plan for the worst-case scenario. If you don't have the money right now, my recommendation is to either (a) get aggressive really quickly or (b) save the money first before you enter real estate.

Figuring in Taxes

One quick word about taxes. As a real estate agent you are an independent contractor (somebody who's self-employed), and your taxes are different than when you're working for somebody else, as when you're in a nine-to-five job, for example. When you're working for somebody else, all you see every month, or every other week, whatever it might be, is your check. Now your check has already had taxes taken out of it, so you haven't really been hip to how the taxing works. But as a self-employed person, not only are you paying federal and state taxes, but you also have to pay Social Security taxes as specified in the Federal Insurance Contributions Act (FICA). As a self-employed person, you need to pay taxes quarterly. And you will be paying the complete amount of Social Security taxes you owe as an individual (working for someone else, your employer would pay a portion of the tax).

Here's how it works. Every quarter you're going to pay Uncle Sam however much you estimate you will owe for that portion of the year's income. In your first year, paying taxes is pretty easy. You can pay very minimal taxes, because there's no projection. But after that first year, the Internal Revenue Service (IRS) is going to look at what you did the previous year, based on the previous year's tax return. And who's to say that you will make the same income one year as the next? I strongly recommend you talk to an accountant about this matter *before* taxes are due.

That's what you *should* do. But what do most real estate agents *actually* do? They pay all their taxes on April 15. They don't make their quarterly estimates, so they end up paying penalties at year's end. As a result, they pay more to Uncle Sam. They're also hustling the first quarter of every year so that they can bring in enough money to cover what they think they will owe come mid-April. I do not have to tell you how stressful this approach is and how poor a model it is for running your business. Don't do what most agents do. Pay your estimated taxes.

A Factor to Consider: Average Commission per Sale

In order to finish the business plan in more detail, you need to find out from your broker-manager what the average commission per sale is.

First, you need to know how a transaction is broken up. Whenever you have a house sell, there are two sides to the contract. There is the seller's side of the contract and there's the buyer's side. Let's assume that there are two real estate offices—two real estate agents who are involved in this transaction. One of them will represent the seller's side of the transaction, and the other the buyer's side. The total commission that's being charged will get split between the two sides. And then, within those two offices, the agents get their piece. For the sake of this example, let's assume you would receive $4,000, in your pocket, for your side.

This illustrates why listings are so important. If you were to sell a buyer one of your listings, you would be getting both sides of the contract. The average side, the listing side or the buyer's side, would pocket $4,000. If you were doing both sides, you would be getting $8,000 for the same transaction. That's great. But let's say all you did was work with buyers. You never worked with listings at all. The most you could ever make in any real estate transaction your whole career would be just that one side. So you need to focus on getting listings.

Now that you know what your average commission is per side, you can determine how many transactions you need to do a year to take in the amounts that you need to take in. You know you will receive $4,000 per transaction. Do the math. Take $100,000 income and divide it by $4,000. You need to do 25 transactions in a 12-month period. In other words, you need 25 houses to sell through you.

Let's assume that this business is all going to be from listings only—and you should stick with listings. Now let's take the 25 sales you're going to do in 12 months and divide that into 12; that's 2.25 sales you need to make each month. (Again, assume you are working with sellers only, with listings.)

This is a nice, average number: 2.25. But not all the sellers who list with you are going to sell. Some of the listings will expire. There might be many reasons for this. Maybe the sellers changed their minds. Maybe they thought that the home was overpriced. Maybe they decided to stay put. Maybe a job offer fell through, so a relocation wasn't necessary. There could be dozens of reasons. In any case, use the rule of thumb that 75 percent of the people who list with you will actually wind up selling. So, if 75 percent of the people who list with you actually sell, you need to get more than 2.25 listings every 30 days. What do you need to get? Do the math. It comes to 3. If you have three sellers list with you every month, 2.25 will wind up going into contract and, based on a $4,000 commission per listing, sold side, you'll make $100,000. This is the Business Plan for Dummies, if you will.

This is a simple example; details can get a lot more complicated. In short, your goal is to get three listings a month. Now, obviously, if your average commission per side is $2,000, which is half of $4,000, you'll need double the numbers. Instead of getting three listings a month, you'll need to get six. And vice versa. If you would like a simple business plan form to fill out, go to www.NewAgent Success.com.

Personal Considerations When You're Starting Out

When you're starting out in the field, you need to think about you and your family (if you're lucky enough to have one) and how the work will affect all of you. You need to consider the following issues and plan for them.

Working Part-Time versus Working Full-Time

One of the questions I always get from people who are starting out in real estate is, "Should I go part-time or full-time?" If you had a choice, my choice for you would be to go full-time, because full-timers can succeed at real estate much more quickly than part-timers can. But some people may not be in the financial position to go full-time. They have to start part-time because they need to have another job to help them survive financially while they get their real estate careers up and running. Depending on what that other job is, there are inherent challenges with that arrangement. If you are working Monday through Friday, nine to five, how much time can you put into part-time real estate? The weekends? The evenings? If you're married, have children, or both, that's going to be tough.

It's not impossible, just tough. But if you can work well with the time that is given to you, you can be a successful part-timer. I've heard of cases where the part-timer did better than the full-timer. Success depends on the individual.

If you're going part-time, you definitely need to focus just on listings. I've said time and time again that you should be focusing exclusively on listings anyway. But full-time agents sometimes choose to break away from listings and take buyers out just to break up the routine. Part-time agents don't have this luxury; they shouldn't be working with buyers at all. Why? Because with buyers, you physically need to be with them in the car and showing property. But if you were working with sellers who had committed to you and hired you to market their house, you could do a lot of marketing at night. Also, while you were working your nine-to-five job Monday through Friday, other agents in the Multiple Listing System could be showing your property. So, you could be earning money in your real estate job while you were doing your other job! That's a pleasant benefit.

Helping Your Family During This Transition Period

Don't kid yourself: real estate is not a nine-to-five job. You need to put in long hours and make some sacrifices to do well. And your family can face difficulties and challenges as you put in the time to make your career succeed. If you let it, this business can consume you; it can become your life. I've seen that happen to many agents, and their family lives suffered as a consequence.

If you are intensely focused on this business (and you often need to be in order to get ahead), make sure that it is on a positive level. Don't become wrapped up in your work to the exclusion of all else; don't become a "workaholic." Here's what Donald Trump had to say when someone mentioned that people considered him a workaholic: "I don't see myself as a workaholic, because what I do, I don't see as work. I just really, authentically, enjoy and love what I do, and that's why I do it a lot, most of the time." That may be your attitude as a real estate salesperson, too. And it will certainly keep you inspired and driven. But you've got to balance your love of this business with the love of your family, because they undoubtedly won't have the same affection for it as you do. The paragraphs that follow will show you how to strike the balance.

Having an "Overview" Conversation

You need to explain to your family how hard things are going to be at first. As will happen with any new profession that you start, you're going to be out of balance. You'll need to put in extra time at the beginning—which means you'll spend less time with them. So, I think you should sit down with your family and give them the overview of the situation.

Be sure to share with them that with real estate you can eventually make a six-figure income—and with relatively little upfront expenditures for education and training. Think about it: in what other professions can you make six figures? Two of the most popular are the legal and medical professions. Folks in these fields have two things in common. Number one, they are going to spend tens of thousands of dollars in education up front. Number two, they need to put in a lot of time, at first, to become successful. Doctors need to do an internship. (I've known of some interns who have actually had to sleep at the hospital because of their shifts.) And attorneys starting in a new firm have to put in some serious hours in order to prove themselves. Even lawyers with their own practices at first need to put in tremendous amounts of extra time, money, and energy to develop those practices: scouting locations, getting clients, developing staff, and so on.

That doesn't happen in the real estate profession. There's a lot of work, to be sure. But you do not have to spend over $100,000 in education to become a real estate agent. In fact, education costs are just a few hundred dollars (costs vary, depending on what state you intend to do business in), and you might need only 30 to 60 hours of instruction. So, you can reap huge benefits from comparatively little money up front.

Monetary expenditures are minor; time expenditures are not. If you truly want to be a successful agent and make six figures, you are going to have to spend a lot of extra time your first year out in this business. Your family has got to be prepared for that. Of course, you don't have to work such long hours. You can come into real estate your first year and work part-time, 20 or 30 hours a week. But the income that you make is going to correlate with the energy you put in. The first year is the most important one. As in any business, it's the time when you set the boundaries and the foundation. It's a critical year. The more hours you put in, the better positioned you are to become a success.

Setting Goals with Your Family

Involve your family in the process of making goals, and make sure that the goals you set have specific rewards for them. Let's examine two important types of goals. The first goal would be what I call your Next Level. This is a vision that is bigger than who you are at this very moment; this goal should take at least a year to five years to achieve. For example, you might want to open up another business, go back to school, pay off some debt, get a house that's twice the size of the one you have now, or buy a brand-new car and just write a check for it. To help you stay focused on your Next Level, you can use the Vision Board. The Vision Board is a board (usually a poster-board) that represents the things you'd like to accomplish for you and your family. What I suggest you do is get some magazines, such as the *Robb Report* or *Money Magazine,* and cut out pictures that represent the things that you would like to accomplish. Then glue the pictures onto the posterboard. I know this may sound a little hokey, but it's interesting to see how this really does work. I have a Vision Board in my office, and my students who have implemented the Vision Board swear by it. I think that what you need to do to help your family members deal with potential frustration during your new career is to sit down with them and set some goals. Then take those goals and place them on your Vision Board.

But you need to have some more immediate rewards for your family. Obviously, a Vision Board of something that you're going to accomplish in the next year or two is not going to help them in six months when you're working six or seven days a week. So your second type of goal is short term, as long as six months or as short as 30 days. It could be to go on a vacation or perhaps to buy something special for your spouse or your children. Whatever the goal may be, place a dollar amount on it and then create one of those "thermometer" charts like the ones you've seen in high schools during fund-raising drives. The thermometer charts show how much money the schools have raised. Students color in the charts with red markers as they get closer to the goal. I recommend that you do the same thing and hang the chart up in a place in your house where everyone can see it. That way, you and your family can follow the progress on the chart and get all excited about it. It becomes a game.

Setting a Schedule with Clear Boundaries

As I said, real estate can suck the life force out of you if you let it. It's really important that you set a schedule with clear boundaries that you never cross. Let's use a real-life story as an example. One of my good friends used to be a real estate agent. He sold over 100 houses a year for five years in a row. The amazing thing about him was that he never worked on a Sunday. To me, that's just incredible, because Saturdays and Sundays are the busiest days of the week for real estate agents. But he was also very faithful to his religion and committed to his family. So, Sunday was reserved for God and for his family, and I have the utmost respect for him. You need to set up the same kind of limits for yourself—and don't cross them!

Your personal boundaries might include one day a week that's reserved for family time. It might be that you're always home for dinner. It might be a date with your spouse every Saturday at 8 p.m. Or it might be Little League practice on Tuesday nights. Hold these boundaries sacred and demonstrate your commitment to your family.

Nothing is foolproof. You may do everything that I've said up to this point to help you and your family achieve balance in your lives, and still you may get out of whack. The next suggestion is a fallback to help you with this challenge.

Creating a Family Fun List

When tension does occur between you and your family (and, unfortunately, it will from time to time), there's one thing you can fall back on to help relieve the stress. I've seen this work for agents and their families countless times. What you can do is create what I call the "Family Fun List."

What's involved is just listing fun things that are very inexpensive and that you can all do on an hour's notice. Such things might be visiting a museum, going on a picnic, playing miniature golf, bowling, riding horses, walking in the park, and riding bikes. (For a sample of things to include on a Family Fun List, check out my Web site: www.NewAgentSuccess.com.) Post this list in a visible place, perhaps on the refrigerator. Whenever you feel that there's a time when the family needs to do something together, just go to the Family Fun List and choose an activity.

Here's the most important part of the game: when you do something on the Family Fun List, you are not to repeat it until you have done all the others. What's great about this concept is that it forces you to be creative with your family and to do new things.

I recommend that when you do something mentioned on the list you highlight the item on the list instead of crossing it out. This way things will pop off the list, and you'll see all the things that you did accomplish instead of seeing things that you didn't accomplish (as you would have seen if you simply crossed the items out).

If you have young children, you'll cherish the times you spent doing things on the Family Fun List; I certainly have cherished the time I've spent with my son. Doing the activities on the list will give both you and your children memories that you'll have forever. You will also be making a positive impact on their lives as well as on your own. Look at the Family Fun List as a kind of Memory-Making List. Keep that in mind as you come up with ideas for things to do— plan for memorable moments. And be sure to bring your camera with you.

Not Putting Your Home or Personal Number(s) on Your Business Card

To really separate your home from you business work life, you need to be careful about the people you give your numbers to and which numbers you give out. Do you want all your personal numbers on your business card so that people can call you at all times of the day or night? What if someone contacted you about business at 11 p.m., after the family was asleep? How would your family feel about that?

One way to handle this situation would be to set up a separate telephone line in your house and have that be your business line. I would avoid giving out a home number entirely. The best thing to do is to have a cell phone and accept your business calls on that. But be careful. The more numbers you have printed on your business card, the more you're making yourself accessible, which can be both a good and bad thing. In my opinion, you've got an office, you've got a telephone number, and you've got voice mail. That's all you really need. If somebody needs to reach you, he or she can leave a message for you at the office, and you'll check the messages on your terms, on your time, versus theirs. Some office phone systems are set up so that every time you call in or each time somebody leaves a message on voice mail, it will actually page you so that you know immediately that you have a call. Consider that option.

Using a Daily To-Do List

There's one final thing to do when you're starting out—and do it yourself. It is an important habit to establish early on, and it may be a no-brainer for you, but if you're not already making and using a daily to-do list, do so. Get in the habit of sitting down every day and writing a list of things you need to do for the day. The best time to make up the list is at night before you go to bed, to clear your head. This is a crucial technique to help you stay focused.

Now that you've estimated how much money you need to get underway in the real estate business and have planned for how to balance your business and personal life, you are ready to find out some specifics of the industry. To learn about the type of people you will meet in this business, what types of businesses there are, and the things you should investigate in the company you are considering joining, turn to Chapter 3.

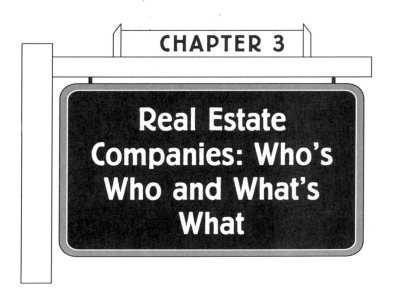

CHAPTER 3

Real Estate Companies: Who's Who and What's What

At this point, you need to familiarize yourself with basic terms of real estate that apply to ownership. By the time you are done with this chapter, you should have a good facility with the major lingo and know what's involved with the different jobs and responsibilities.

Realtors and the National Association of Realtors

Let's start off with a term you might have heard before: *Realtor®*. It seems as if over the years the term *Realtor* has become synonymous with *real estate agent*, but the two don't mean the same thing. A Realtor is a member of the National Association of Realtors. You can get your real estate license and still not be a Realtor. You can practice real estate and everything else and still not be a Realtor. But almost every licensed agent—I would estimate 90 percent of them—are members of the National Association of Realtors (NAR).

The NAR organization is broken down into states. And it's further broken down into a local Board of Realtors. Even though the NAR is a national association, you join at the local level; when you do so, you automatically become a part of the national group.

There are so many benefits to being a member of NAR. There's a monthly magazine, plus annual conventions you can attend. It's really a no-brainer to become a member of the association. If I'm not mistaken, if you work for a broker who is a member of the association, you have to become a member yourself, as an agent. So it's really not a choice.

It will cost you between $300 and $400 a year to join, but it's worth it. Fees will vary, depending on where you join. Every state association and local Board of Realtors has different pricing.

You can join as a Realtor or as a Realtor-Associate. Usually, the Realtor is the broker-owner or the person who owns the real estate company. The Realtor-Associate would be the agent; that would be you.

Through the NAR and the state and local boards, you are tied in to the Multiple Listing Service, which is one of the best tools for a seller to get her or his house sold. (See Chapter 5 for more on the Multiple Listing Service.)

An added advantage to being with the National Association of Realtors is that it has, and all its members are sworn to, a Code of Ethics regulating their behavior. Most buyers and sellers, and certainly all agents, are familiar with this Code, and it guarantees not only a built-in level of fidelity to the client on the part of the Realtor but also ethics in everyday behavior. Sellers know they can trust you. For more information and to see the actual code, check out www.realtor.org.

People at the Real Estate Company

The people you are likely to meet at a real estate company include the person who owns the company, usually called the *broker of record, owner, president,* or *principal.* Depending on the size of the company, you may also encounter a *manager.* This is somebody designated to run the office; it doesn't mean that he or she owns the company. And then there's the *salesperson,* also referred to as the *agent.*

The Real Estate License

Before you can practice real estate in the state in which you want to do business, you need a *real estate license*. Every state has its own process for getting one, so I will limit myself to describing the process in one state, in general terms. For a list of all the state Web sites and what is needed in order to receive your real estate license, go to www.NewAgentSuccess.com.

Let's use New York as an example for how to go about getting your license. In the Empire State you need to take a class that is 45 hours long. Some schools in other states can cover the same material in a week or even in a couple of days. Others, elsewhere, can take as long as a month. But in New York you take your 45-hour class. Then, you would actually take a test. Before you take the test, though, you need to indicate on the test itself or tell the people at the test site which broker you're going to be working for. So, in New York it makes sense to first find the real estate company for which you're going to work, then go through the 45 hours of education, and then go for the test. Once that happens, you're licensed, and the broker holds on to your license because you're working under his or her umbrella. Anything that you do reflects upon the broker. If you get caught doing something illegal, you are in trouble, and so is your broker.

Types of Real Estate Companies

There are many different types of real estate companies. I've broken them down here into five general categories. These could probably be broken down even further, but here are the five most popular ones.

Mom-and-Pop Company

The first category is commonly referred to as the *mom-and-pop* company. The mom-and-pop office is usually one where the broker-owner is still listing and selling real estate. He or she doesn't have a separate manager. These types of operations have fewer than 20 agents in their offices. They are not part of any kind of franchise. So it might be something like Bob Smith's Realty, a very small company—a boutique shop. The advantage of this type of company is that it's hard for you to hide. The broker can always motivate you and get you to work hard. It can be a very positive atmosphere. It's intimate. You don't get lost in the shuffle.

For example, when I started in real estate, I started in a mom-and-pop office. The company I was working for at the time had maybe 10 or 12 people, tops. I was young and living on my own, since my dad passed away when I was 14. At 19, I was the only boy in the office. The women in that office (and they were all women) became like a surrogate family to me. They were all looking out for me and taking care of me. It was good for me at that time in my life to have had that kind of support.

Large Independent Company

The second category is the *large independent company*. This type of company, which is not part of a franchise organization, is solely owned and has at least 100 to 200 agents. Some large independents have over 2,000 agents. (I know of one that has over 10,000!) The good thing about a large independent is that there is a tremendous amount of money coming into that company because it has so many agents and so much market share. What's really positive about that situation is that the money can be funneled back to the agents in advertising and in the local market. These large independents focus their energy, their money, and their resources in the market that they want to own. They are not spread out too thin. But there is one disadvantage: you can get lost in a large company unless the manager is a great one and is very hands-on. With a large independent you will find a lot of synergy and energy. There's very much a large-family feel to it.

Franchise

The third category is the *franchise*. Some of the most popular franchises are Century 21, Prudential, Coldwell Banker, ERA, Better Homes & Gardens, Realty World, and GMAC. A mom-and-pop office or a large independent can actually buy into one of the franchises—and no longer be independent. With a franchise, you can tap into the power of the national exposure that that company brings. The other things a franchise provides you with are training, education, name recognition, and perceived value, to name but a few. There's a great argument to be made that, when someone hires your company, he or she is actually buying into the whole franchise nationally; that perception benefits the seller. So there are some advantages to working with a franchise.

Unlike with the other two types of companies—the mom-and-pop operation and the large independent company—with a franchise, part of your commission will go toward the national advertising budget that the franchise has. Those costs do eat into your profit a bit, but the argument could be made that the money you'd be paying for advertising would go back to you in business that you wouldn't have had if you weren't a part of the franchise.

Discount Broker

The fourth category is the *discount broker*. A couple of franchises—for example, Help-U-Sell and Assist-2-Sell—are focused solely on the discount broker. Here's how discount brokers operate. They offer limited service to sellers, and because they have limited marketing, they can charge sellers lower fees than some of the other companies. So, let's say the average commission in a market is 6 percent. Discount brokers might have commissions of only 2, 3, or 4 percent. What the discount brokers are trying to do is attract sellers based on something other than the marketing that they do or on something other than market share. They are trying to attract the sellers based purely on price. That is the main focus of this model. An analogy would be the difference between going to a doctor and going to a clinic. If you went to a doctor who specializes in what ails you, you'd be getting thorough treatment. A clinic would charge less, but you'd be getting fewer services. A discount broker is like that clinic. The full-service broker who is charging the higher commission would be like the doctor who specializes.

100 Percent Company

The fifth and last category is the 100 percent company. A couple of franchises that you would recognize would be RE/MAX and Realty Executives. To fully understand how a 100 percent company operates, you need to know how an agent gets paid.

Every real estate transaction has two sides: the listing side and the selling side. The selling side is the office and agent who brought the buyer to the property; the office that listed the property would be the listing side. So, you would take 100 percent of the commission and split it in half between the two sides; 50 percent goes to the selling office, and 50 percent goes to the listing office. The agent of each office shares his or her percentage with the broker. So let's say you've got a $10,000 total commission. Five thousand dollars goes to the listing office; five thousand goes to the selling office. Let's say that each agent in both offices is on a 50-50 split with his or her broker. That means each agent is going to get $2,500, and the broker of each office gets the other $2,500. That's the model across the board for commissions and how agents get paid.

With the 100 percent model, the payment is handled like this. The selling side still receives half of the $10,000 total commission: $5,000. But the agent in this model would keep the full amount. He or she would not share that $5,000 with the broker. (Sometimes the amount might be divided a bit, so the agent would keep, say, 95 percent and the broker would get 5 percent. But, for all intents and purposes, it's still the 100 percent model.)

Sounds like a great arrangement, right? But you're thinking, *wouldn't the broker have to be paid somehow?* She would. With the 100 percent model, how the broker gets paid is by actually charging each agent rent. In such a situation, you'd be paying a set amount of dollars to the broker every month—say, in this case, $800—whether or not you have any money coming in. You also have to pay all of your own expenses—all of your own advertising, all of your own supplies, everything. With the other models that I mentioned before, that wouldn't be the case. In those other models, because you're splitting 50-50 with the broker, you are considered to be in a partnership with her. So everything, more or less, gets divided in half.

Which model is better? I don't think you, as a new agent, should work for a 100 percent company for the simple reason that you don't have any money coming in and you already have a bunch of overhead. If you go into a situation where you've got to pay rent every month and pay all of your own expenses, you're just getting into deep debt.

You'd be much better off working for a broker where there's a partnership. The better you do, the better the broker does, so he or she has a vested interest in your success. In the 100 percent model, there isn't that same commitment to you, because the broker receives rent from you whether or not you take in any money. There are exceptions to the rule. Some 100 percent companies and brokers in the office are very supportive and very committed. But you'd be better off not risking getting into debt.

You could negotiate your terms with a 100 percent company. I've seen this happen many times. For example, a representative from the 100 percent company says to an agent, "What we'll do is waive your rent for the first six months while you build your business. We'll run an ad for you, and we'll get you some business cards." I've seen some 100 percent companies actually start new people off at 50-50 and give them the opportunity to work into 100 percent. My theory is if the 100 percent model works, then the 100 percent model works, and those brokers should just do the 100 percent. Why start an agent off with 50-50 and try to do all these different models?

One more thought about the 100 percent model. Usually, the agents who work at these types of companies are somewhat different than those in the other types of models. Because they're paying rent, paying their own expenses, and managing their own money, they bring a business mentality to their work. That's great. But I've found that there's not a lot of nurturing or support for the new agent in the 100 percent office. A new agent needs to ask people questions, to lean on them, to shadow them. You don't usually find a lot of that activity going on in a 100 percent model.

To sum up, of the five models, the one I would recommend to a new agent is the mom-and-pop operation, a large independent, or a franchise that is not a 100 percent model. You can always work in one type of operation first and change to another later. There are still certain requirements and areas of importance that you need to look at, regardless of the model, and I'm going to share those with you now.

Items to Consider When Investigating the Right Company for You

So, you're attempting to choose the right company to work for. What are the specific areas you need to look at when making this decision?

The following are the things you need to take in consideration, listed in what I feel is their order of importance.

Market Share

The first thing to look for is what the company's market share is. To calculate that, use a simple equation. Just take the total number of houses currently for sale in the market and divide it by how many of those listings are listed with the company. For example, if 1,000 houses are currently for sale and the company has listings for 112 of them, it has a 11.20 percent market share. There are two ways to get this information. First, you can ask the company to share it with you; the other way is call the local Board of Realtors. If you need the phone number for your local Board of Realtors, go to www.New AgentSuccess.com.

You also want to find out if the company is a big listing office. You want to work for an office or company that is a leader in the marketplace when it comes to homeowners listing their houses for sale with agents. There are a few ways to get this information. You can check with the local Board of Realtors; you can check the Multiple Listing Service, if you have access to it; or you can check with another agent.

But there's another great way to find out. Simply ask a representative of the company: "What is your market share as far as listings are concerned?" Now that's a great question, because the company has to tell you. If the broker or manager you are speaking with doesn't tell you, it's probably because he or she doesn't know. That tells you something about his or her leadership style. Brokers or managers should definitely know what their market share is. If they don't, they are not good leaders; they don't have the right focus. If they do know and they don't share it with you, it's because they're embarrassed at the market share. In either case, it's a great question to ask.

(Note: Unlike corporate America, where you go on a job interview, you meet with an interviewer, he or she asks you questions, you respond, and eventually you hope to get hired, in real estate, the agent, the interviewee, is usually the one who's leading the interview. Why? Because the broker-manager has difficulty with determining whether or not an agent is going to succeed. There are plenty of times a broker-manager looks at somebody and thinks, *boy, that person doesn't have the look*. He [or she] doesn't interview well. It doesn't look like the person being interviewed is going to succeed, and then all of a sudden, he or she surprises the heck out of you. So brokers and managers, I think, tend to hire people who are interested in real estate. They figure, *let's see how they work out; if they don't work out, then we'll let them go.* So, in effect, you, the agent, are the one who needs to ask questions and raise concerns during the interview. But don't come across as if you are conducting the interview; don't appear to be arrogant. Be respectful. Know that you have the right and the duty to yourself to ask questions so that you can decide where your career is going to start.)

You also want to determine if the production a particular office generates is coming from just one or two agents. Here's why this is important. Let's say the office generates a lot of business, but 60 percent of that business is by one agent. There are two problems with this situation. First, that one agent, no doubt, is *really* running things. History shows that when agents have that much control they start pushing their weight around. Of course, any brokers who work in that office would succumb to that agent's "demands," because if they didn't, they would they stand to lose a lot of revenue. The second problem is that if that agent left the company, the office dynamics would change dramatically; you wouldn't recommend the office shortly after taking that kind of hit.

Training

The second thing to look at is training. What kind of training does this company do? If you're interviewing with an office that's part of a large independently owned company, you can be fairly certain that there is training. All the large companies actually have their own in-house trainers, their own training directors, who run this kind of thing. So, that's a big plus for these large independents. The mom-and-pop office may have its own in-house training program, which it created itself. And the franchise organization will most likely have training. Over the years, franchises have really moved toward the online type of training, where you do it over the Internet, which is not the same as a live class. Keep in mind that agents say they get a tremendous amount of value out of a live environment. You want to determine what the commitment of the company is to training. And find out what kind of training is available in the office. Does the company do hands-on field training? If so, is it franchise training online or company training?

Going to a classroom and learning a number of things is great, but you want something that helps you "where the rubber meets the road," where it really counts in your day-to-day job. So, you need to find out if the office does more training than simply "here's the light switch and here's how to turn the copier machine on and off." What kind of training in terms of listing and selling skills does the office have? Some offices have monthly seminars for which they bring people in. Sometimes they have weekly contests. Contests aren't training, but in a sense they are. They may have brainstorming sessions. So you really want to look at that in-house stuff. Actually, ask to see a copy of a company's training manual, if it has one.

Location

The third item to check out is the location of the office. Although the location is important, it's not as crucial as the two items previously mentioned. Nevertheless, it should be investigated. What I suggest you do is drive into town and look at the real estate offices that "pop out" at you based on where they are situated. Check to see if they have ample parking. Are the offices visible? Let me tell you about Mac Levitt, the broker I used to work for. When Mac first opened his office, it consisted of him; his wife, Pat; his daughter, Carrie; and myself. That was it; the whole office consisted of just the four of us. And our first location was in Mac's house. We never brought clients or customers to the house, so we'd always meet them at the local diner. Within the first six months of us being "open," we became the number-one listing and selling office in that marketplace (the "office" being, of course, Mac's house). Then, when we actually moved to a storefront, there was no front parking. Really, if you were driving more than five miles an hour, you would miss the office. So Mac, even to this day, never had a great location, but he is a great salesperson. That's why the training you receive and whether the office is a big listing office are more important to me than location. If you have got the skill and technique required for listing and selling real estate, it doesn't matter where your office is located. Still, location is a factor that needs to be considered. You must evaluate all things.

One last thing about location. It's better for you if the office is near your house. If you have to drive more than a half hour one way to your office, that's just going to be a pain in the neck. I've heard some agents say, "Well, I'll just work out of my house." That's fine if you're a self-starter and don't need an office environment. More power to you. In that case, you might as well work for a 100 percent type of company because you're not looking for an office synergy atmosphere. But a long haul to the office brings up time management issues. After all, you're going to have to go to the office periodically to drop off contracts, to pick up forms, to get yard signs, and to do dozens of other things.

Environment

The fourth item for consideration is the office environment. When you walk into this office for this interview, how does it feel? Does it feel busy? Is the reception area clean? What's your desk space going to be like? How do the people use technology? Are they big on technology or not? These are the things to look at. Something I recommend as far as an office environment is concerned is to get there about 20 minutes before your scheduled time. If you've got a two o'clock appointment, get there at 1:40. If you're in luck, you'll catch the broker or manager off guard. He or she won't be prepared for you, which is what you want. So, you can sit in the reception area for about 20 minutes, watching and observing the whole feel of the office, getting a sense of it. And you will.

You'll be able to determine whether you like it or not. Also, you should be talking to the front-end receptionist. Ask him or her a few questions. Probe a little bit. For example, you could ask, "How long have you been working here?" High turnover rate for office assistants is a telltale sign that the broker or manager is not a good leader. Find out how long the assistant has been working there.

You can also ask, "Do you like working here?" You can tell if the answer you get is an honest one or just a stock answer the person gives because he or she is afraid that the broker may be listening. You can tell when somebody's being authentic.

A couple of other questions to ask are, "How many agents are in this office?" and "What's your market share?"

Also, you want to find out if the broker or manager actively lists and sells real estate. You know that in the mom-and-pop office the broker is going to be actively listing and selling. But I'm not crazy about a broker or manager who's talking to sellers, listing property, and showing houses for two reasons. Number one, if the broker-manager is listing and selling real estate, she is not managing, leading, and training agents. So, every time she is out there doing her own business for herself, she is not there in the office taking care of the team. Number two, there's a sense of you, the agent, competing with the broker or manager. Obviously, the broker or manager would have an advantage over you as an agent when push came to shove on anything. Nevertheless, I have seen some offices that have handled that situation successfully. For example, the manager may list and sell, but he still takes the agent with him on an appointment to either learn or to share the listing with him. This situation is not impossible. But, unfortunately, as a new agent, you won't learn whether this arrangement really works out until you're already there. And I'd rather you go into an office knowing all the answers and starting your career that way versus taking the trial-and-error approach. After all, this is your career we're talking about.

Promotion

A fifth thing to look at is what kind of promotion the office does. How do you know that an office is doing a lot of promotion? Just look at what you're getting in the mail at your house. Are agents from the office knocking on your door? Are you getting mailings from the office delivered to your house? When you open up your local paper, are you seeing ads from the company that are bigger than ads from other companies? If you look at yourself as the consumer, what comes to your home? Of all the companies that are around my area, one company sends me more material than any other company does. That's a great sign. Also look at the print advertising the company is doing. You can look in your local paper or go to the supermarket and pick up the real estate magazines. Do they have small ads or ads that just show their agents and no listings? If they don't have full-page ads of listings, it's probably because they are not a big listing office. Look at the promotion.

How Leads Are Handled

A sixth thing to investigate is how the office handles leads. For example, with listings (remember, sellers are preferred over buyers), somebody wants to list a home for sale. When the person calls in, who does that call go to? How is that potential listing managed? Does it go to a rotation? Does it go to the agent who is the top-producing agent? The same thing applies to buyers who are calling in. If buyers call in and want to buy a house, how does that get handled? One of the popular models in handling both scenarios is called uptime–floor time. That's when you sit at the desk and wait for the phone to ring. Don't do floor time; it's just a waste. For you to make the six-figure income you want, you need to get on the phone and knock on doors. Do proactive things. Sitting in the office waiting for the phone to ring is not proactive.

The kind of office that you, as a potential listing agent, need to look for is one that rewards the listing agent and in some respects penalizes the other agents. For example, if you have a listing and there's a yard sign, and a buyer calls in on the yard sign, that buyer lead should go directly to the listing agent, which in this case would be you. That's great. That's the type of broker and office that you want to work for, one with that kind of mentality.

Commission Split

The last thing to look at is the commission split. As mentioned earlier, the traditional split of the commission is 50-50. (I've never seen a model where the agent gets less than 50 percent.) For example, if there were a $10,000 commission, half would go to the listing side and half would go to the selling side. So, each side would receive $5,000. Let's say you're the listing agent. Your percentage of that $5,000, if you were receiving the traditional 50 percent split, would be $2,500.

It might seem odd to have the commission split be the last thing you investigate; after all, most agents look at the commission as the highest priority item; after all, it's how they are paid. So why look at it last? Let's say you go into an office that says it will give you 85 percent of the commission. Sounds great, doesn't it? But the broker could perform badly, conduct little training, and have terrible market share. What's the point of having a large share of nothing or next to nothing? Eighty-five percent of nothing is still nothing. I'd rather you get 50 percent of something. Here are the different types of approaches that companies use to pay their agents:

100 percent commission. Companies that pay agents 100 percent (some pay 95 percent but call themselves 100 percent) expect the agent to pay a flat fee every month. Plus, the agent pays for all of his or her own expenses: letterhead, yard signs, advertising, and so on. With this model, you pay your monthly desk fee regardless of whether you generate money that month or not.

Graduated split. This is relatively simple concept: you first start off at a set split, and as you generate sales, your split increases. For example, you may start at a 50-50 split. After you hit a certain number of "gross closed commissions" (the total number of commissions you have generated and received for the office before taxes), you may increase to 55 percent, and the broker receives the remaining 45 percent, and so on.

Graduated split rollback. This split is just like the regular graduated split, except at the beginning of each year you start off at 50-50 again. Therefore, you have to "prove yourself" again and again each year.

You're now ready to tackle investigating which real estate company would be the right one for you—the topic of the next chapter.

CHAPTER 4

Choosing the Right Company, with the Right Training, for You

What's involved with the job interview? What questions do you need to ask to determine what company is right for you? What do you need to find out? Before delving into that, let's examine some things you need to take into account before the actual interview.

The first consideration is what impression you need to make. Above all, be yourself. The chance of a broker hiring you is very good, unless you have done something terrible. It's not that brokers have low standards, it's simply that, as I said earlier, they really don't know if you're going to succeed or not until you have already tried. So there shouldn't be a lot of pressure on you. Don't feel as if you have to wow them. It's more the other way around. But don't be arrogant; be respectful. Don't come across like, "Yeah, I'm the big cheese here and I'm interviewing you." If you do come across as arrogant, they won't want to hire you because they won't like you. And they do need to like you. The second consideration is whether the broker you interview with seems organized. Look at how the people at the company present themselves. For example, a broker or manager who sits down with you and gives you a history of the company will create a positive impression. That person might tell you where the company came from (meaning its past), where the company is at present, and where the company is planning to go in the future. If you see that kind of orchestrated presentation, that's great. You want to see a person selling you on the company, because if that broker or manager is a great salesperson in this meeting with you, there's a good chance (but not necessarily a guarantee), that he or she will help you to be a good salesperson in the business. If that person is doing terribly in this presentation, most likely he or she will be a terrible leader. (The truth hurts, doesn't it?) If you don't have the talent to be able to sell your company, and if you don't take the time to actually come up with a presentation, you won't be a good leader.

Another consideration is how the company you interview with compares to others. I definitely recommend that you interview with a minimum of three companies. Why? Because each time you go on an interview with a broker in another office, you're learning more and more about the business and what questions to ask. By the third appointment, you'll be on a much stronger footing than you were on the first two. So do it to learn as much as you can about the real estate industry in general and your area's real estate market in particular.

Another consideration before you interview with a company is whether the office has a written polices and procedures manual. Ask whether it has one. To me, having such a manual available is really important, because there will then be something to refer to in case there are challenges and in-house bickering (and there will be). Its absence would be sorely felt. For example, let's say a buyer calls in and you get the call. You show him the property and he buys the property. All of a sudden, another agent in the office says, "That was my buyer. I already took him out and showed him the property last week." What happens here? Some offices would say that the two agents have to share the commission. Some offices would say that the protesting agent did not do a good job keeping her buyer. If she did, the buyer wouldn't have gone to this other agent, so she doesn't get anything. Whatever the policy or procedure is, it shouldn't have to be made up on the spot. There should be a written policy and procedure for this and similar situations.

Another consideration is whether the company you interview with has a Web site. If it doesn't, that could be a red flag. A company with its own Web site shows a level of commitment, a level of leadership, a level of business mentality, and a level of tech savviness.

When you investigate a company's Web site, you should look at the link that tells about the company (it's usually called "About Us" or something similar). Click on that link and read about the company's history a little bit before you go to the interview so that you know what you're walking into. See if the broker or manager knows the information on the "About Us" page as well as you do. It would tell you something if the broker-manager didn't. Another thing you should do is to search Google. Go to Google.com, type in *real estate* and the name of your town, and see what company names come up first in the list. That should at least tell you which companies have a strong presence in your area.

The last consideration is floor time. If you can, find out before the interview what the company's policy is on floor time/floor duty/uptime (there are different names for it). Basically, this involves you being designated, on certain days and/or times of the week, to be available to answer the phones and handle any calls that come in. I am not a fan of floor time. I think it's the office assistant's or receptionist's job to answer the phones. If a broker says it's mandatory for you to do it, then to me that's a big strike against the office. So check this out beforehand; if you're unable to find out this information before the interview, then definitely ask the broker or manager during the interview whether floor time is part of your job.

Keep in mind that you don't make money on floor time. Now, you *can*; but you usually won't. The broker or manager is almost sure to tell you that you can make money on floor time: "We get a lot of calls that come in, and there's a lot of activity and a lot of plusses to handling the calls." That's what you will be told, and the broker or manager will believe that. But, trust me, that's not the best use of your time. You're not going to make $100,000 sitting there waiting for the phone to ring.

If a broker or manager tells you that floor time is optional, that's a different story. That's fine. It's not bad to have the option of answering some calls. Maybe once in a blue moon you will even want to take a call. But mandatory floor time is something to be avoided.

Questions to Ask on the Interview

Now it's time to examine some of the questions you should ask when you go on the interview. (By the way, when you go there, you should dress nicely; dress to impress.) When you're sitting across from the broker or manager, and after he or she is done with the presentation about the company, that's when you ask your questions. You should do so not only out of respect but also because it will give you an opportunity to observe that person and see how she or he leads the conversation. Plus, some of the things that the broker or manager will share with you will definitely bring up new questions that you'll want clarification on later. Also, as the broker or manager shares information about the company, he or she may answer some of the questions you already have.

Here are some of the questions you need to ask:

What kind of administrative assistant support does the office have?
Most offices have an administrative assistant who handles miscellaneous things and answers the telephone. In some offices, the assistant provides a great deal of support. For example, if you get a listing, you give it to the office assistant and he or she inputs it into the Multiple Listing Service. The administrative assistant also handles the placement of ads. With contracts, the assistant might do some follow-up work. Some offices call this type of assistant a "sales coordinator." Find out as much as you can about the support staff. When you have an assistant who gives you a lot of support with the business, it makes life so much easier.

How long has the current administrative assistant been here?
If the current administrative assistant has been at the office for only a couple of months, find out how long the previous assistant was there. Why ask that question? It will give you a good idea of the level of support you are likely to get and the type of turnover the office experiences.

What's the agent mix?
Find out the number of full-time and part-time agents who work at the office. When you ask how many agents the

company has, you need to know how many of them are active, full-time agents. Keep in mind that some people get an education, take the state exam, get their license, and then hang that license in a real estate office because they have to display it, but they're actually not actively listing and selling. So an office could have 30 people with licenses but only 20 full-time agents actually doing the selling. You want to know what type of mix will be in the company you're interviewing with.

What are the goals of the company?
What does the company want to accomplish over the next 12 months? What you want to hear the broker tell you is not just about market share for the company, but what its growth potential is. If you hear the broker say, "Well, we're at 20 agents; we want to grow to 40 in the next 12 months," that tells you something very solid about the broker. It says that the broker has goals of growing the office, which is a good thing. If the company is committed to growth, that benefits everybody.

What technology does the company use?
Some agents in the office may have better and more technology than the company itself has. Therefore, you need to find out what technology the *company*, not the individual agent, has in place.

Does the company have a mentor program?
Most likely, the company you are interviewing with doesn't have a mentor program, but ask anyway. If it doesn't, see if you can set one up, because you've learned about it from this book. Later in the chapter, I will explain in detail how the mentor program works; see "Finding Your Real Estate 'Buddy.'"

What is the company policy on agents investing in real estate?
You certainly should have the desire to start investing in real estate. Your goal should be nothing too large; just two or three properties. Regardless of what the company's policy is about this type of investment, you should be looking for

this: if you should buy or sell anything for your own personal gain, whether it's for you to live in or for you to own the property and rent it or flip it, the company would get no commission. That arrangement is unlikely to be what the company's policy is. The common policy is that when you buy something, the commission that is part of the buying side would go back to you. But when you list and sell it, you actually pay a listing fee. There may be some kind of reduced format for you buying and selling for investment purposes.

To clarify, suppose you work at Bob Smith's Realty and you're buying a listing from XYZ Realty. Naturally, XYZ Realty has to get its percentage of the listing side, whatever that is. You don't have any control over that portion of the commission. But on the buyer's side, you would hope that the broker would not take a portion of it. You would get 100 percent of the broker side and the salesperson side. The reason why is that you can use this commission to help offset some of your expenses in buying the property. The same thing applies if you're on the listing side. You don't want to pay anything to your broker-owner when you're buying or selling real estate. As mentioned, for anything that's with another company, that company will have to get its percentage. It's unlikely that the broker will agree to this arrangement, but you want to shoot for it anyway.

You should explain to the broker up front that you don't have any desire to buy and sell a lot of real estate. That's not why you're getting into the business. But tell him or her that for the occasional investments for your own personal gain, you should have the option not to pay any fee.

Are there any restrictions on self-promotion?
You need to find out what restrictions, if any, the company will put on you and your efforts for self-promotion. For example, can you have your own Web site? Can you have your picture on your business cards, for-sale signs, both? It's really good if a broker encourages and allows you to put your own face on all of your promotional materials and doesn't have

any major restrictions. Some companies have restrictions; others don't and actively encourage agents to promote themselves. In all of your promotional materials, you have to have the company logo and the company name. That's a legal thing; you always need to promote the company. But find one that has some freedom for you to promote yourself as well.

How are the incoming calls on listings distributed?
As already discussed, how are the calls on an in-house listing handled? Do they go to the listing agent, or do they go to the general pool of agents? You want calls to go to the listing agent.

What is the average income of the active agents working in your office?
A broker may have to really think about how to answer this. It's a great question because, as mentioned in Chapter 1, there's a rule of thumb that says your income should be the average of that of your five closest friends. If you're in an office surrounded by other successful agents, then you will rise to the occasion and become one of them. The aura of success rubs off on you. If the broker-manager is hip, he may know what you're asking and why, so you've got to weigh his answer. If you're lucky, his answer will be nothing but honest. But he may attempt to justify whatever answer he gives; he may tweak the number and still consider it to be true. For example, he may give you the average of the top five active agents. Meanwhile, the office has 20 agents, so what about the other 15? Remember, you're asking about the average income of *all* the active agents in the office. If you feel that the broker-manager is not being straight with you, then probe some more. Ask a different question to get at what you want to know: "Well, that's based on exactly how many agents? Your top 10 or 15? What about the rest?" Find out this information before you accept a job with the office.

That's it. Those are the basic questions you should ask at the interview. Let's move on to the topic of working with a Real Estate Buddy—a mentor. How does that work?

Finding Your Real Estate "Buddy"

Whatever real estate company you decide to go with, it should have a mentor program of some sort. The program companies use to conduct training in real estate is sometimes called by different names, usually "field training" or a "mentor program." I choose to use the term *Real Estate Buddy*. The reason I do so is because I was inspired by my son. In school, whenever he and his classmates leave the classroom, for a field trip or whatever, they have to hold hands with their buddies. To me, that's what I envision with agents training in the field.

A Real Estate Buddy is another agent in the office who you work with and who takes care of you. She or he is the person you can go to for answers and who can help you with real estate transactions. As already mentioned, you should be buying audio programs and attending live seminars and training courses, and that effort is great. But training in a classroom, at a company, at a hotel, online, or wherever is not quite the same as when you're actually out there in the field, listing, selling, and working with buyers and sellers. You need some kind of support system.

The type of mentor program that is in place in a particular office may influence your decision as to whether to work there or not. As mentioned, always ask whether the company you're interviewing with has something like a Real Estate Buddy Program available. If it doesn't, ask the broker-manager if he or she is willing to work with you on establishing one. I would be shocked if any broker would oppose education and training for a salesperson, especially a new salesperson. This is essentially what the Real Estate Buddy Program is.

The reason it's important to get a Real Estate Buddy is because it is extremely unlikely that the broker or manager will be training you and working with you. She will be there for general questions and general support. But even if she is really hands on and is working with you in some respect, you will still learn much more from a fellow agent who is actively listing and selling real estate. Why?

For starters, you'll feel okay about bugging your Real Estate Buddy whenever it comes to the silliest or most important thing. You will have questions, and the broker or manager may not always be around to answer them. New agents usually feel very uncomfortable posing questions to their fellow agents in an office. The new kids on the block are usually afraid that they are going to be interrupting the long-timers or that the questions they have are stupid ones. What starts to happen is that new agents feel uncomfortable, and this impedes their effectiveness. If these agents stop asking questions, they don't learn.

Your Real Estate Buddy, because of the relationship, is going to be rewarded in monetary terms for working with you. Because your success will benefit your Buddy financially, you should have no qualms whatsoever in asking her or him as many questions as you need to. After all, you can't be a success without asking questions.

The second reason why you will learn a lot from the fellow active agent is that she or he will be there to help negotiate your first few transactions. What you learn in a classroom is totally different from what happens in a live situation. With your Real Estate Buddy right there next to you, you'll get help with those first few deals—and with whatever tricky situations may arise.

The third benefit to working with a fellow active agent is that he or she will be able to help you generate listing appointments. Make sure your Buddy is someone who is not afraid of listings and who's strong at listings, which will help start you off in the right direction.

The fourth benefit is that the active agent, your Real Estate Buddy, will actually go on listing appointments with you. When you go on the first few listing appointments to talk to homeowners about hiring you, no matter how much you've been trained, it's going to be very scary. Your Real Estate Buddy will be there helping you through the conversation.

What's Involved in the Real Estate Buddy Program

Let's examine the things you and your Buddy will do and the relationship you will have in the Real Estate Buddy Program. One question you might have is, "How long do I work with this Real Estate Buddy?" The answer: until you feel comfortable that you can do your business on your own. You'll be the judge of when that moment will be, but I'll make a suggestion about how you can decide. As mentioned, you need to focus on getting listings. So, use that as the focal point. As soon as you get four listings and two sales (even though I recommend that you not show houses in the beginning, you probably will do so on a very small scale)—sales where you have taken buyers out and they have bought through you—that is when you will no longer need to work with your Real Estate Buddy. Or it could be that after you've gotten your fourth listing with your Real Estate Buddy you're on your own.

What's your relationship with your Real Estate Buddy? Who's responsible for what? Here's a general overview of how it would work.

With the first listing that you get together (keep in mind we're going to go for four), you will generate the listing appointment yourself, you will go the appointment together, and your Real Estate Buddy will deliver the whole listing conversation to the seller. Once the homeowner hires both of you, the Real Estate Buddy does all the servicing—writing the ads, doing the broker's open house, and so on. The Buddy will spend all the money in promoting that listing. You will tag along and basically be like an assistant for the Buddy on that particular listing. That's the way you're going to learn this business out in the field.

With the second listing you get together, again you get the listing appointment yourself, but this time you do the servicing yourself. You'll split the expenses 50-50 with your Buddy, even though you're doing all the work. Your Real Estate Buddy will be there for support. If you have questions about how to do something, he or she will be there for you. The Buddy goes on the listing with you and does most of the listing appointment.

With the third listing you get, you'll again generate the listing appointment and you'll both go on the listing appointment, but now you should do all of the talking and marketing.

With the fourth listing, you do everything yourself. The Real Estate Buddy really doesn't do anything. You get the appointment. You go by yourself. You do the servicing. You spend all the money. Your Buddy is just there, basically, so that you can ask questions of him or her.

You're going to pay your Real Estate Buddy on each one of these listings, but the payments will change as the responsibilities shift— and they are going to. In the beginning, the first listing, with the exception of you getting the appointment, your Real Estate Buddy is doing most of the work; therefore, he or she is going to get most of the commission when the house sells. With the fourth listing, you're doing all the work. But your Buddy is still there to support you, so you'll give your Buddy just a little bit. With your fifth listing, you're totally on your own, so you don't share anything with anybody except your broker.

Obviously, you're never always on your own. Everybody in the office is there to support one another. But I think whatever agreement you and your Real Estate Buddy start off with, you personally need to stick with it. So, if around listing number 2 or 3, you feel that you don't need your Buddy's help anymore, you should still do the right thing. And whatever your agreement was, say, if it was to go four listings with her or him, then that's what you should stick to.

If you include responsibilities for buyers in this job description between the two of you, generally you would do everything with the buyers. You yourself select the houses, take buyers out, show buyers the properties, and so on. Your Real Estate Buddy is only going to be there to support you and answer simple questions, because working with buyers is easy (and it's compensated accordingly).

You show buyers property. If they like it, they'll buy it. And it's not quick money. It's not the best money. It's like anything else. You get what you pay for based on the difficulty of the job. The more talented you are or the harder it is to do a job but you do it well, the more you get paid. That's listings. Working with buyers is very easy. You'll select the houses, take the buyers out, and you'll show property. Now you're going to ask your Real Estate Buddy which houses you should show them. You'll just ask the basic question, and your Buddy won't be investing a tremendous amount of time, because he or she is only answering you, not showing property. When you take buyers out, if they like a house, you're going to have to write a contract on it. You're going to have to present that contract to the homeowners. Your Real Estate Buddy will be there for you. The best thing is that, on the first transaction, or even the second one perhaps, your Real Estate Buddy presents the whole thing for you and you just watch, listen, and learn.

Who Gets Paid What

How does the Real Estate Buddy get paid, and how do you get paid? Based on what the broker pays you, you're going to take a percentage of your pay and give it to your Buddy. So, for example, let's say that the average total commission for a sale is $10,000. As mentioned earlier, half of that goes to the listing side of the transaction and half of that goes to the selling side. So, there's a split of $5,000. Assuming you're on a 50-50 split with your broker, and it was your listing that sold, of that $5,000 that you split with your broker, the broker gets $2,500, and you get $2,500. On that first listing, what you're now going to do is take your $2,500 and pay 75 percent of that amount to your Real Estate Buddy, which is $1,875. That means that you keep 25 percent, which comes to $625. Now, when you look at that, it may not seem like a lot of money, but keep two things in mind. First, this is just your first transaction, and, second, if it weren't for your Real Estate Buddy the transaction might never have happened in the first place. Once again, this distribution is the best thing you can do to start your career off the right way.

On the second listing, after the split of the commission between you and your broker, you will share your portion equally with your Real Estate Buddy. So, carrying through the amount from the previous example of $2,500, you would pay yourself $1,250 and the Real Estate Buddy $1,250. On the third listing that sells, you would get 75 percent of that $2,500, or $1,875, and the Buddy would get 25 percent, or $625. And on that fourth listing, that last one you would have to share with your Real Estate Buddy, you would get 90 percent, or $2,250, and your Buddy would get just 10 percent, or $250, because you're doing everything. You're listing it, you're marketing it, you're spending the money on it, and so on. You're just giving your Buddy 10 percent as compensation for serving as a support system, someone you feel comfortable with and can go to with questions. As far as the two sales, you can simply give your Real Estate Buddy 20 or 25 percent of those first buyer sales that you do. I think 20 percent is fair.

You can change these numbers, but the concept is that there has to be enough incentive for the Real Estate Buddy to work hard and to be involved with you. For that to happen, you've got to pay him or her well. That's one thing I've learned; it's important to pay people well. At my company, I like to think that I pay my folks really well. That way if I'm ever a jerk, they'll be more forgiving of me because I do the right thing with their salaries. I've seen some brokers pay terrible wages to their support people, and what do you think happens? They have a huge turnover in staff. They can't seem to keep anybody for more than a little while. If you want somebody good, you've got to pay him or her well. It's possible that the Real Estate Buddy you pick could be on a higher split with the broker, because not everybody is at the same split. An agent's individual split is based on her or his production level; the better the agent, the higher the split she or he receives. So, if you find an agent you would like to work with and the split is 75 percent to her and 25 percent to the broker, then I would put those first four sales under the Real Estate Buddy's name. That way, the commission is getting paid at a higher rate. Then you can split the commission, and it works out better financially for you and for your Real Estate Buddy. Naturally, the broker has the final say on this. If you are a broker reading this, it's a good concept to pay it out this way. This is your contribution to these two agents to help this new agent get trained the right way in the early months of his or her career. Find out what a homeowner really wants when he lists with you and several ways to get your listings sold fast at top dollar in today's changing market.

Selecting the Perfect Real Estate Buddy

How do you select a Real Estate Buddy? You can ask your broker for recommendations.

Obviously, you do not want a low producer. But I don't neces- sarily think that the top producer in the office should be picked either. The reason is that the model a top producer uses for running a business is very different from that used by the average agent. Top producers have more money, more resources, and more name recog- nition. Basically, they have a lot of the things that you, as a new agent, do not have. You can't really use their type of business as a model and emulate their behavior.

The best type of agent to be a Real Estate Buddy would be a decent agent, an average agent. He or she would be in the middle of the production level in a particular office, wouldn't be afraid of prospecting (that agent might have apprehensions about it from time to time, but for the most part, he or she is strong at it), and would get a good number of listings. That's what you want.

If all goes well, the broker has given you the names of a few agents. (Be sure to have her give you more than one name, because you should be the one to make the final decision.) Then have a conversation with each agent. Do not explain the Real Estate Buddy idea yet. I want you to do a little investigative work, as if you were a news reporter, and ask these questions.

What did you do before you were in real estate?
This will give you a good picture of the person. Why did he get into real estate? Did he get into it because he was born into it? Because he had family members who were in it? Did he do it for independence, or did he do it because he was part of a witness protection program with the government? This should tell you a lot.

How long have you been in real estate?
Ideally, you want someone who's not too new to the business yet not too long in it. Anywhere between one year and 10 years would be great.

What is the best way to make money in real estate?
So, what do you think I think she should say in response? Yes, "getting listings." If she says anything other than this, you should move on and find another Real Estate Buddy.

How are you at listings?
Find out what his production level is. How does he react to that?

How do you feel about calling For Sale By Owners?
If the person is a little nervous or uncomfortable about it, I don't have a problem with that—and neither should you. If she has a strong aversion to it and is totally against it, I would pick another Real Estate Buddy.

What do you think is the biggest challenge I will face, and how should I handle it?
The answer will give you a little insight about the agent and show how he would deal with a crisis. But most importantly, it's actually a little bit of a rapport builder. It's just a useful question to ask, I think.

Once you've asked those questions, I would go right into asking the agent if he would be a Real Estate Buddy if you asked him to be. What follows is a probable dialogue between you and the agent after you have asked the questions.

You: *I went to the broker and asked her, "Who is the best agent, in her opinion, that really knows this business better than anybody else in the office?" And you know what? She gave me your name. The reason I asked that is because I wanted to make sure that I learn this business the right way and the quickest way possible. And I thought that having somebody I can be partners with on a short-term basis would be the best way to do that. So, here's what I want to ask you. If I got a listing appointment, would you go with me? I would pay you for going with me on that listing appointment.*

Agent: *Oh, yeah, absolutely.*
(We hope this would be the response, and it should be.)

You: *Well, okay, that's great. I read in a book about a Real Estate Buddy and how to set it up. The book had a great way to do it. So I'd like to go over that with you and make sure that it works for you.*

You would then propose the commission split that was mentioned earlier. Once you've had that conversation, then the last thing would be to ask the agent:

You: *By the way, can I go with you on a couple of the appointments that you get on your own, where I'd just be a fly on the wall?*

So for any listing appointments that this agent actually gets himself, you would go along on them just to listen and learn. The agent should not have a problem with this, because he will benefit financially from you becoming a stronger agent.

You are now well versed in how to approach the job interview, ask the right questions, and get the information you need to help you reach a decision about which company to work for. Next up is getting focused on *yourself*, to find out the best system for making it all work for you.

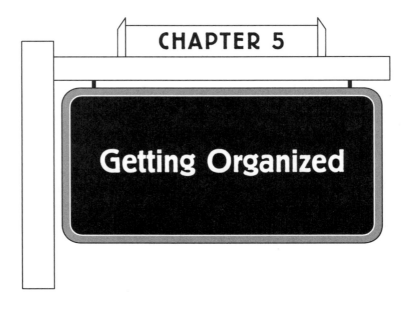

CHAPTER 5

Getting Organized

You are familiar with the different types of real estate organizations. You know how to find the right office, choose the right broker, and find a Real Estate Buddy. So now you're ready to start sinking your teeth into this business. It's time to learn how to get organized.

Why Organization Is Important

One of the reasons why businesses fail is because they fail to plan. They fail to set up good systems, to be organized, or both. There's a great book out there called *E-Myth Revisited* by Michael Gerber (HarperCollins, 1995). He says that all successful companies design a business that is system-dependent, not people-dependent. Obviously, you need people to perform the job, but the system itself should be strong and not solely dependent on the skills and abilities of the people running it.

Suppose I told you that there was a business where all the employees were teenagers, there was a high turnover, and even the managers were teenagers. It wouldn't sound like a very good business, would it? But that's just what McDonald's is: a bunch of young people (for the most part). They make hamburgers and other food that always looks the same and tastes the same, because they have a system. And how successful has McDonald's been?

You need to have good systems in place for your business. And the key to that effort is organization.

An Organization System for You and Your Money

The first thing to have well organized is your money. Make sure that you have a good system in place for managing your own money and your own expenses. The best way to do this is to use financial planning tools such as budgets, income statements, bill paying systems, and the like. For a list of some great financial planning tools, go to my Web site: www.NewAgentSuccess.com.

A huge concern, from early on, is to take care of your retirement. It's important that you get into the habit of putting away something for retirement every month. The best way you can set yourself up for a comfortable retirement in later years is to use some kind of brokerage account where money is automatically taken out of your paycheck. You should look at making a retirement payment on a regular basis as being just as important as making your regular monthly mortgage or rent payment. Another way to set up money for your retirement is to invest in something, preferably real estate.

If you're married and have children, you'll need to set aside something on a steady basis for your kids' college expenses. Again, you can have a fixed amount taken out of your paycheck on a regular basis (every month, biweekly, whenever you get paid). A great Web site to check out is www.Upromise.com. You register all of your credit cards with this organization, and whenever you use one of your credit cards at an establishment that has an agreement with Upromise, a certain percentage of that bill (1, 2, 3 percent, whatever) actually goes into a 529 College Fund Account for any child you choose. It doesn't have to be your child. It can be your grandchild or friend's child; it doesn't matter. This is a great—and easy—way to put aside money for future college expenses.

Things You Need to Be Organized

To be well organized in business, you need to have the right equipment and supplies. Let's examine some of the things you will need. (If you go to www.NewAgentSuccess.com, you will also find a whole slew of links to help you in this area.)

You need a computer of some kind. I recommend you get a notebook computer, because it's portable. You can bring it on listing appointments with you. You can take your work home very easily. You can carry it on vacation with you. There are a bunch of companies from which you can order a computer, but the company I like the best is Dell. That's because it has great support and great computers.

You also need a color printer. You'll need this to print out the packages that you are going to put together for sellers: brochures and informational 8½-by-11-inch documents that are put in a small binder you can get at Staples. Forget the inkjet printers; you can get color laser printers very inexpensively. (Remember, laser printers produce much better quality documents than inkjets do.) If you get a Dell computer, you can lease a color laser printer at the same time. Maybe it'll cost you about $100 a month to have a laptop and laser printer.

You should also get contact management software. This helps manage your leads and your schedule, which in turn will help you stay focused. There are a couple of great companies out there that sell this type of software. Once again, go to www.NewAgentSuccess.com for a list of these companies.

You'll definitely need a digital camera. Now, you won't need it your first week, but you'll find it to be very useful on the first two listings that you get. With a digital camera you can take internal shots of your listing and create a virtual tour. You can take a photo of the listing before you go into the house and upload it onto your laptop and show the homeowner what the home flyer would look like. So, a digital camera is very important; it is also an inexpensive item nowadays. You can still get $1,000 digital cameras, but the one that you would need would probably be $300 or $400 dollars tops.

A good photo of yourself is essential. Make sure it's a professional-looking shot. Don't go using beauty pageant photos or high school headshots from when you still had hair. Use an updated photo of yourself, don't airbrush the picture or doctor it up in any way, and be sure to wear nice clothes.

Nice outfits are important. When I got into real estate at the age of 19, I could afford only one suit. And that suit was what I always wore when I went on listing appointments. I wore that sucker out in, like, 60 days. I don't know what your money situation is, but always be dressed for success, and if you can afford only a couple of outfits, then just keep rotating them. Women have the benefit of mixing and matching accessories to make things look different. Two outfits can be made to look like 20. And men can change ties to give themselves different looks.

You ought to be driving a good car. It's not important to be seen in a Mercedes, and you don't have to have a brand-new car; a nice, decent car will do. One of my students tells a story about when he first got into real estate. He called his first car the Flintstone Mobile. The reason is that it had a hole in the floorboard in the front of the car, and you could actually see the road as you were driving. If he pushed too hard, his foot would have gone through the floorboard. But after his first year in the business, he put it (and himself) out of its misery and bought a brand-new luxury car. Which car do you think made a better impression?

Make sure you stay within your means. All of the things I have mentioned are not mandatory. Do only what you can afford to do. Don't get overwhelmed if you can't do everything you think you should. For example, making your own stationery is a good thing to do, but it's optional. Most likely the company that you work for will provide you with business cards, letterhead, and envelopes, so you'll have them without having to pay anything. But if you have the financial means to create your own brochure, your own letterhead, your own envelopes, and your own business cards, you can create some jazzy pieces. Some companies will charge you thousands of dollars to create these things. To me, that's just ridiculous. You don't need to spend that kind of money. I know some companies where it will cost you only $500 to $600. Again, go to the www.NewAgent Success.com to see a list of those companies.

You want something to help you stay organized beyond just your laptop notebook—some kind of portable device. A Palm Pilot can be very useful and very powerful.

Buy a tape measure for your listing appointments. You can use either the newer electronic kind or the old-fashioned kind.

Thank-you cards are a great thing to have because they are inexpensive prospecting tools. Along the same lines are showing postcards, which essentially are cards you leave behind at the house after you have shown it to a prospective buyer if the homeowner isn't there. Instead, you could leave your business card, which is what most agents do, but a showing postcard has a little bit more information that you can fill out. Use of a showing postcard is more professional than use of a business card. For a sample of showing postcards, check out www.NewAgentSuccess.com.

Another item that is very helpful is a yellow map. These are little yellow telephone books published for just one, two, or three towns or neighborhoods. They come with maps that are dedicated just to those areas. Whatever you call it, you need to get a map of only the market that you're working. Using such a map will make it a lot easier for you to learn your market. If you have a mapping feature in your car, then you don't need one of these maps. Your car's map is sufficient.

As a safety measure, you should have a good spare tire in the trunk. You'll be amazed at how many people don't have one.

You should also get a membership in the American Automobile Association (AAA), which is a great organization. Membership is just $40 to $50 a year, and it really makes sense for a real estate agent who spends a lot of time in the car to have it. You'd be surprised to learn how many benefits you can get from being an AAA member, among which are emergency road assistance, travel discounts, and automobile insurance.

Some agents find a tape recorder to be good tool; it can record any thoughts or questions you may have as you're learning the business. But I'm not a real fan of tape recorders. The reason is that you've got to sit down and listen to it to transcribe it. Why take the extra time? I prefer to just write everything down in a spiral binder.

You ought to have a number of things available in your car at all times for clients' needs. You should have things that kids might enjoy or that can entertain them—for example, a little toy or a coloring book. Also, moist towelettes like Handi Wipes are useful in case your clients get their hands dirty from touching something in a basement or if the children have a chocolate bar melt in their hands. A couple of umbrellas should be nearby: one for you and one for your clients. And, last but not least, have a box of tissues handy for those times when people are so emotional that they start crying when they finally find the house of their dreams.

The last thing you need to get, as far as equipment or supplies go, is a mailing house or a person to do your mailing for you. When you start doing mailings, you should have a company that you know—or somebody in the company where you're working—to help you out. So, all you have to do is call up that person or company and provide the information about what you want mailed. They will have your letterhead and envelopes, and they'll print your mailing, stuff it, and send it. In other words, they will do everything for you. You do not want to be doing that kind of thing yourself.

Superior Filing Systems

Organization is almost impossible without the right kind of filing systems. Basically, you should have three simple systems for your files: filing for the market, filing for sellers, and filing for buyers.

Filing for the Market

The first type of filing system is filing for the market, to learn about that market. (Learning your market is a topic we'll discuss later in this book.) And what is this system? This is going to sound really silly because it's so basic and so simple, but the system is just a spiral-bound notebook like the kind college students use. You're going to use this notebook when you preview homes to help learn your market. The broker I worked with, Ann Dictor, taught this technique to me. As odd as it seems, using a notebook really makes a big difference.

To learn your market, you need to go out there and preview homes. Doing so can very quickly overwhelm you. To overcome this, Ann suggested I do this: "Darryl, as you go through a house, just write in a notebook every room that you walk into as you go through the home." So, for example, after entering by the main door, when I walked into the foyer, I would write "foyer" in my notebook. Then when I walked into the living room, I would write "living room." (You can use abbreviations instead of writing the entire room name, whatever is easier.) Then I would walk into the next room, the kitchen, and write "kitchen," and so forth. Now, doing this may seem ridiculous, but, let me tell you, it made a huge difference. I probably looked at about 20 homes this way, and afterward, I didn't have to do it anymore. This technique helped me to remember those homes.

The other thing that Ann taught me to do is to write in this notebook the address and the name of the homeowner at the top of the page. The most important thing Ann told me is that after going through the house, write something to help you remember that house. For example, if the property had an incredible backyard, write "incredible backyard." If it had some kind of cat smell, then write "cat odor." If the furniture seemed like it was more expensive than the house, then write "Donald Trump furniture." The important thing to do is to write some key words. They will help you remember the property and its features. This type of filing system will help you get a feel for the market.

Filing for Sellers

Another filing system is for sellers. There are two types of sellers. There's the kind who actually lists a home with you and becomes a client. And there's the kind who is a lead, somebody who you are trying to get to list with you.

Filing for Clients

Filing for a client is very simple; just make up a very simple manila folder with the client's name on it and put that in a file cabinet. Every time you have notes, correspondence, and other written communication pertaining to that client, just put it in the folder. If all goes well, as your year progresses, you're going to have so many sellers that you're going to fill up that file cabinet.

A lot of real estate offices have a contract folder that you could use to store this type of material. Usually, the contract folder is reserved for when something goes into contract. But I've seen some agents use that folder for storing their current listing information. Eventually, you hope, the listing is going to sell, so there won't be a need to make two different folders.

If two folders are necessary, how can you distinguish between the folder for a listing and the folder for a seller who actually went into contract? I simply put a different colored dot, or some kind of marker, on each one to mark what kind of folder it is. Of course, you can always make up a separate drawer for each type of folder: one drawer for current listings in contract and the other drawer for sellers who haven't gone into contract yet.

Filing for Leads

Filing for leads is handled differently. Your company might have a system that it uses to manage the listing leads, but what I'm about to teach you is very popular with my students. It's called the FSBO (For Sale By Owner) File Box. Here's how it works. You cut out the For Sale By Owner ad from the newspaper and put it on a three-by-five-inch or a four-by-six-inch index card. You write in the upper-left-hand corner the town where the house is actually located; that information will be in the ad. In the upper-right-hand corner of the card, you write the telephone number that is in the ad. You also want to find out the address of the property, which most of the time isn't given in the newspaper. In order to get the address, you have to do what's called a *reverse lookup*.

Reverse Lookup   A reverse lookup is where you supply the phone number, and whatever search system you are using—be it a book, CD, Web site, or whatever—looks up the address for you. A normal information search would be for you to call 411 and give them an address or the name of the person, and they give you the phone number. In this case, you have the phone number but not the name of the homeowner or the address, so the search is done in *reverse*.

There are a couple of ways to do a reverse lookup. Some offices have computer software that does it quite easily. You can also do a reverse lookup by going to a Web site such as www.411.com. Another option is to purchase a CD or book from a company called Cole Directory (www.coleinformation.com/html/RealEstate.aspx). This company publishes a book of all the addresses in a given town, for which you pay an annual fee. You simply look up the phone number in the book or on the CD, and it tells you the name of the owner and the address of the property. That's why it's called *reverse*.

Why look up the address? Well, the town is big; it has subdivisions. You want to know where the property is located so you can do some comparisons. For example, suppose you see a newspaper ad stating that there's a "four-bedroom, two-bath colonial in the town of Hunna-Hunna." You look up the address, 1010 Umpty-Ump Lane, and now you know that it's a four-bedroom, two-bath colonial in a certain neighborhood. Either you really know the neighborhood well already or you can investigate it. Then when you look at this ad you can tell if the house is overpriced or if it has a fair price. It's just good knowledge for you to have before you call the homeowner. That's why it's important to reverse it.

When you call a homeowner (and you'll find out in Chapter 7 the dialogue you should use on calls to For Sale By Owners), you will not use this information. For example, you would not call and say, "Hello. Mrs. Hunna-Hunna? This is Darryl Davis from Power Realty." She'll get defensive right away and say, "How do you know my name?" So don't use the name, and don't use the address. Just do the lookup for your own information.

Filing the Card for Leads   By this point you have cut out the ad, taped it onto an index card, reversed it, and written out the address and name of the homeowner on the front of the card. The upper-right-hand corner is the phone number; upper-left-hand corner is the town. Furthering your efforts to prepare things for the FSBO File Box, you're going to write notes on the back of each card. Whenever you call on people, if you don't get in the door, follow up on the call; record the history of calls on the back of the card. Now, how do you actually file the card? You take the card and you put it in an index box. You can buy index boxes that have the tabs 0, 1, 2, 3, 4, and so on. File the card by the last four digits of the telephone number. The reason you file by the last four digits and not the first three is because, as you know, most towns have what's called a prefix. So the prefix is the same for most of the houses. If you filed by the first three digits, your box would be very heavy with certain numbers. Doing it by the last four numbers spreads the cards out a lot better.

Instead of using index cards, you could have a filing system consisting of 8½-by-11-inch sheets of paper. You can even create a form; good examples of templates you can use for these forms are on my Web site: www.NewAgentSuccess.com. The good thing about the 8½-by-11-inch method instead of the index cards is that you can also easily file entries for houses that expire from the Multiple

Listing Service. When those expire, they will become new leads for you. I find the use of a three-ring binder to be preferable over index cards for keeping track of leads from the expired listings. The only advantage to using the cards is that, because they're smaller and more condensed, they're easier to carry around in your pocket if you want to. But using them becomes a problem when you start working the expireds, which I also want you to work with.

Filing for Buyers

The last filing system is for your buyers. Most offices have some kind of buyer sheet or buyer card: a form you can use that has the name and address of the buyer, what style of house he or she is looking for, price range, qualifications, and other information. Ask your broker for that form. How do you file it? That's the key. A lot of agents file it by the *person's name*. I want you to file it by *price range*. The following example illustrates why you should do so. Let's say a house comes up for sale. You've taken buyers out, you've shown the property, and they haven't bought. All of a sudden, a new listing comes out that's a hot house in a particular price range. It's easier for you to find the right buyers if your file system is organized by price range. Say that you've got a $500,000 house that just came on the market with another agency or with you (it doesn't matter, but it's a good house for $500,000). You can easily find which buyers say they'll buy something around $475,000 to $525,000. This system is a lot easier to organize and use.

To Be Digital, or Not to Be Digital?

All the types of file systems I've described probably can be in digital format, especially with the listing leads and with the buyers. But as tech savvy as you think you are (and I am), I would recommend that you stick to the tried-and-true methods: paper, pen, notebooks, and binders. Why? Because technology isn't the answer to everything. When it doesn't work, you're in trouble. When was the last time you lost a few days because your hardcopy notebook crashed? Never. With hardcopy materials you don't have to boot something up. You can stay focused on the page. The paper and pen method is a lot easier to use and a lot more reliable than the electronic method.

Another advantage to filing hardcopy materials is that the ads and information you clip can tell you a lot about the homeowner. As you read the For Sale By Owners ads that you've cut out and saved, you start to develop an instinct about them. A particular ad can tell you how important the homeowner (or seller) considers the listing to be. How many lines did the ad take up? Did the homeowner use bold typeface or not? Also, when you look at an ad, you can remember the property, if you've called these people before, or if you've seen the ad before. When you go digital, it takes away the visual aspect of all this. I think that the salesperson instinct develops when you see a real hardcopy ad.

Dot Board for Listings

Another filing device is not really a file system but a motivational tool. It's called the *Dot Board for Listings*. Now if you read my other book, *How to Become a Power Agent in Real Estate* (McGraw-Hill, 2002), or if you've attended any of my seminars, you should be familiar with the Dot Board for Listings. Basically, it's a visual chart that you create. Go to a stationery store and purchase some posterboard. It's basically the size of flipchart paper, which you can use to create a poster. Also buy some little sticky dots about the size of a quarter.

To make up the Dot Board, go from left to right, creating five columns: Month, Telephone, Schedule, Attend, and Listings. On the left-hand side, from top to bottom, in the Month column, you're going to write Week 1, Week 2, Week 3, Week 4, and so on. In the next column, which says Telephone, every time you get on the telephone and you actually talk to a homeowner, whether it's a call with a For Sale By Owner, a call with an expired, or a cold calling, you would place a dot in that column. Every time you talk with a person you give yourself a dot; answering machines don't count. You need to talk to a human being about coming over to see his or her house. Whether you actually visit or not, you still give yourself a dot.

Now, if all goes well, this column for Telephone is going to get filled up quite a bit. It all depends on how many columns you can get on a page and how big the space to be filled in is. Once you fill it up, you'll make a new chart. So, the chart probably is not going to go for a full year. Keep that in mind.

Every time you schedule a listing appointment to go see a house, you give yourself a dot in the Schedule column. In every listing appointment you attend, you give yourself another dot in the Attend column. For every listing you get, you put a dot in the Listing column.

Now, this sounds extremely hokey, but let me tell you, agents who have used a version of the Dot Board for Listings love it. Using a Dot Board will help you to stay focused. It will be a motivator.

What's the point? The objective—and the fun—is to get as many dots in the second column, Telephone, as possible. Why? Because the more dots you get in the second column, the more dots you'll get in the third, and then the more you'll get in the fourth, and then the fifth. And that last column, Listings, is where you make the money.

So you need something to keep you motivated and focused. And this Dot Board is going to be a big deal for you. Don't worry about calculating how many dots you need to get in one column in order to equal something in another. You'll learn what your percentages should be as you start using it.

You may not have enough room in your office to hang the chart. Perhaps you don't have a wall that's big enough. Maybe you can ask your broker-manager if you can hang it up in the kitchen for just yourself. Doing so can be a little embarrassing, because all the other agents are going to see your board, but that might be a motivator for you. So, if it is, put it there. Or you could take your Dot Board home. But I like it better in your office, where you're picking up the telephone and making calls. Having it nearby and filling it in as you go is the whole point of this exercise. Not only does it track your production, but it also keeps that productivity figure in your face. So, if you don't have the space in your office for a grandiose Dot Board, then perhaps take the same concept and shrink it down. Make a smaller poster. Get smaller dots.

Utilizing Technology to Get Yourself Organized

Technology can be a great tool in getting yourself organized. So let's look at the technology you should be using. I've already mentioned you should have a laptop, printer, and digital camera. Let me give you some suggestions for the beginner, the average person, and the intermediate user.

For the Beginner

If you're a beginner, meaning you're not familiar with technology at all, then you need to get started. The best place to start is by getting connected to the Internet. That means you have to have an e-mail account. One of the best places to begin is MSN (Microsoft Network). There you can get your own e-mail account, learn the Internet, and start messing around. So get connected. Get online.

Your local cable company may also provide you with Internet service, and if it does, it can give you an e-mail account. So if you've got cable right now, just pick up the phone, call, and tell the cable company that you need to get on the Internet.

You could also get a technical person, a techie—somebody who can help you learn some of the things you need to know and who can also be your troubleshooter. If you have any questions, problems, or situations, you have somebody to call. Your techie could be a friend or family member, who can also help you with setting things up. Or, go to the Yellow Pages and find somebody. Obviously, that'll cost you, so using a friend or family member if you can.

When you first go online, I want you to begin by using Google (www.Google.com). Google is a great place to start learning the Internet. It can direct you to lots of good information on many topics. For example, when a family member came down with trigeminal neuralgia, something painful we were not familiar with, we looked it up on Google (we "Googled it," as they say). We got so much information, we knew more about the condition than most of the doctors we talked to. So if you have anything you want to find out more about, Google can get you the information.

The other thing you want to do as soon as possible is get your own domain name. What is a domain name? Look at it this way. The Internet is like open land, almost like the Wild West was in the 1800s. Maybe not so much now; maybe it's more like the 1900s. The point is that there is a lot of opportunity on the Internet for you. What you should do is buy your own lot—your own piece of real estate on the Internet—your domain name. The most logical domain name you could use would be your name—for example, www.YourName.com. The Web site www.NewAgentSuccess.com will direct you to a Web site that will walk you through the easy procedure for securing your own domain name. The investment is only about $9 a year, and it is definitely worth it.

If your personal name is not available as a domain name, then you want to try and get some other type of name related to real estate. You would first try your personal name, then your initials, even your family name. It's good to have a few different variations. Also, if your name can easily be misspelled, you want to secure the misspelled versions as domain names as well. I made the mistake of not getting my name in several spellings, because my name can be spelled a couple of different ways, and somebody else has a spelling of my name. That situation actually has created some problems.

For the Average Person

If you're somewhat tech savvy, I have some suggestions for things you ought to do. First, start looking into getting your own Web site. Find out how to provide visual tours for your listings, which is a really cool, salable item. Make sure you have autoresponders set up for your e-mails, and that's basically it.

Another suggestion is to take classes to help you become more tech savvy. The Multiple Listing Service probably has classes you can take explaining how to use the service. It may even have some other computer classes you can attend, such as desktop publishing and how to use e-mail. Check with your local Board of Realtors and your Multiple Listing Service to see if there are classes that would help you improve your tech skills. And, of course, a community college may have a class or two for you if you want to avail yourself of their instruction.

For the Intermediate-Level User

For the intermediate-level user, I suggest you get even more familiar with the Multiple Listing Service and the things it can do for you. Let me share with you ways in which you can use this awesome tool to help you get familiar with the market. Although I can't teach you how to use the Multiple Listing Service (every system is different), here are some things to look at once you do learn how to use it.

Listings This Year Compared to Last Year

Check to see if there are more listings this year compared to last year. If there are, that tells you it is a buyer's market. Why? Because of the law of supply and demand. If supply outweighs demand, buyers can be more aggressive in asking sellers to lower their prices; if the sellers don't, the buyers have many other houses from which to choose.

Number of Sales This Year Compared to Last Year

Compare the numbers from this year to last year. This will tell you if the market is on an upswing or a downswing. In a downswing, you will also start to see prices of homes flatten out or even decline.

Average Days on Market

Your Multiple Listing Service most likely has a feature that tells you how long, on average, a house is on the market before it goes to contract. This is your average days on market. If you combine that information with the current average sales price in your area, you can determine the minimum length of time you would want a seller to list a home for sale with you. In other words, if the average days on the market for a house is currently 90 days, you would want a home-owner to list with you for at least 120 days (an extra 30 days, just in case), assuming that the asking price of the house is not too high.

This Year's Sales Price to Last Year's Sales Price

Compare this year's sales price with last year's. This information will tell you the rate of appreciation or depreciation—as the case may be— for a house in your market. So, if the average sales price last year was $200,000, and this year the average sales price is $224,000, the appreciation rate is 12 percent. Keep in mind that houses do not appreciate at the same rate each month. In other words, with this example of 12 percent appreciation in one year, the house did not go up 1 percent each month for 12 months. There are seasons in real estate: winter, spring, summer, and fall. History has shown that appreciation rates go up just before the school season starts, because families want to be settled in their new homes before classes begin.

The Market Saturation Rate (MSR)

The most comprehensive study of them all is the market saturation rate (MSR). This shows the relationship between the number of houses for sale with the number of potential sales, and how long it should take for a house to sell. Let me explain. Suppose that last year in a 30-day time frame there were 500 houses for sale, and during that same 30-day period there were 150 sales. If I take 150 sales and divide it into 500 houses for sale, that would give me a market saturation rate of 3. What does this mean? It means that it should take three months to sell all the remaining houses that are for sale. Now, if this month, a year later, there are 1,000 houses for sale and there are 200 sales, the MSR is 5.

So, even though the number of sales has gone up, the number of houses for sale has increased, creating more competition for homeowners. This means it will take longer for sellers to sell their houses. The only way for homeowners to sell their houses quickly would be to ask for lower prices for their homes than their neighbors are asking for theirs.

Having all this organization in place will impress the people you most want to impress: your clients. It will also help you to be productive. And having all of the information I've discussed here will make you sound much more professional in the eyes of homeowners. It shows them you know your market!

Now you're ready for something really meaty: prospecting.

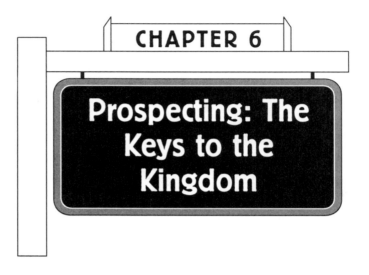

CHAPTER 6

Prospecting: The Keys to the Kingdom

Now you're ready to tackle perhaps the most important thing that you will do as a real estate agent: prospecting. Mastering it can be tricky, as you'll see—but the rewards are great, so the effort is well worth it.

So, let's find out about the important general concepts, techniques, and tips you need to know to really succeed at prospecting. Once you've wrapped your mind around these need-to-know things, you'll be ready to begin your prospecting journey in earnest.

The Importance of Prospecting

The most important thing for you to master to really succeed in real estate is prospecting. Ironically, prospecting is one of the things at which most agents are their weakest. I think this is so because when people first get into real estate they have a misconception about the business. Before they are licensed, when they look at houses with another agent, they think: *Gee, this looks easy. I can do this! I like houses. I like people, most of the time. Yeah, I can do this!* So they get into real estate, and they realize quickly how difficult it really is.

To be really great at real estate, you have to be a good businessperson. You've got to be a self-starter. You've got to know how to manage your business as a business. You need to make calls, show property, negotiate, and so on. There are a lot of skills that are important to being really great in this business.

But the most important skill, as I've said, is the ability to prospect. You can be great at all the other skills, but if you do not know how to generate business, you'll never really succeed.

Most, if not all businesses have to be good at prospecting in some fashion or another. Dentists, lawyers, and cleaners all need to be good prospectors. For example, cleaners may use different forms of prospecting, but they need to have the skill to go out and generate new clients and customers. A cleaner is not going to call up a homeowner and say, "Would you like to clean your clothes at my place?" He's going to do some kind of advertising, such as a direct mail piece or an ad in a paper. Another example is restaurant owners; they may get involved in the local clubs, like the Kiwanis Club or Catholic Charities, so they increase their visibility, give their restaurants a good name, do their civic duty, and encounter potential customers and contacts. There are dozens of reasons why joining these organizations is a good idea.

So, all business owners need to be good at prospecting. They can't just sit by the phone waiting for people to call; it's not going to happen. If owners are bad at prospecting, their businesses are going to suffer. If you've got a restaurant that doesn't advertise, offer specials, get its name out there, press the flesh, do direct mail, or any of that kind of thing, do you think that restaurant is going to survive for long? Of course not! That's true of almost every business.

Stick with Prospecting the Listings

One area where most agents mess up when they get into real estate is to become discouraged and get away from prospecting. They start calling For Sale By Owners, and people hang up on them. So the agents say to themselves, *let me try door knocking.* So they start knocking on doors, and people slam the doors in their faces. After a couple of months of these trials and tribulations, they say to themselves, *You know what? I think I'm going to take a break from prospecting for a while because I wasn't so good at it. I'm now going to work with some buyers. Once I've worked with some buyers, shown some property, and made some sales, then I can always go back to the listings.*

Please listen to me: do not be seduced by the Dark Side of the Force, because that's exactly what it is. First of all, working with buyers does not necessarily mean it's quick and easy money. It may look like that on the surface, but agents who have been in this business for a while will tell you there are plenty of times when you are working with buyers weekend after weekend and they are not buying anything. They may decide to rent, or, worse yet, buy from another agent, and you would have invested a lot of time and energy with nothing to show for it.

If, instead, you took that same energy, that same tenacity, and you applied it to listing real estate, you probably would have gotten several listings that would have equaled thousands of dollars. So, here's my challenge to you: if you are brand new in real estate, before you take any buyer out to show him any property, you need to get six houses, six sellers listed with you. If you do that, I promise you that you will be one of the best and greatest agents in your market. If you can get past that first hurdle, those first six listings, you won't even want to take buyers out. Please trust me on this. As I've said before, listings are where you should focus your time and energy, as they bring the best returns. So, if listings are so important, why don't most agents spend their time prospecting for them? Even the good agents lose their focus from time to time. Why is that? The key to focusing has to do with two things: *excitement* and *passion.*

Let me explain with an example from my life. I am really good at generating and managing my business, writing seminars, creating concepts and distinctions, and a whole lot of things. In other words, I'm great at working the *mental muscle* of my body. But when it comes to the other muscles in my body, I'm terrible. I am not into working out and being healthy. I would much rather go on stage and entertain, train, make people laugh and learn something, or work on the next seminar. I like working the creative part of my body as opposed to working the physical. For the past eight years I've been having a real struggle with this.

Then one day a friend of mine told me: "You know, Darryl, agents look at you and ask, 'Well, if he's not disciplined in the area of his health, how can he teach me to be disciplined in real estate?'" That was an honest question, which got me concerned. So, I thought, if I'm disciplined in my business, why can't I be disciplined in this area? Then I started to think of other agents who are extremely disciplined with their health but are terrible at being disciplined with real estate. So why is that? Why are some of us having problems with discipline in certain areas but not in others?

My conclusion: we are disciplined in certain areas more than others because we are excited and passionate about them. We are committed to having a breakthrough in those particular areas. I just wasn't passionate about going to a gym, jogging on a treadmill, or riding a bike. But what I am excited and passionate about are children. They are full of possibilities. Lo and behold, I found a way to combine my need to improve my health with a way to help children. Not too long ago I learned that leukemia causes more deaths than any other cancer among children under the age of 20. I also discovered that the Leukemia & Lymphoma Society has a program called Team In Training, where they train you for a marathon and all they expect from you is to raise a minimum amount of money. So this inspired me. I thought I could have a personal breakthrough with my health by helping save children's lives. I can get excited about saving lives! As of the writing of this book, I just completed my first half marathon (13.1 miles), and I have just been accepted to run a full New York City Marathon.

So, you need to have excitement and passion for what you do to stay with it and to succeed. Find what engages, fires, and inspires you, and run with it.

Approaches to Prospecting

All agents have different ways of generating their own business. This book will give you a plethora of ideas on how to prospect, and you may go to seminars and hear more. You need to choose the prospecting approach about which you can get excited. Whatever approach you can stay focused on, that's the one you need to do.

The approach that I love the most is calling For Sale By Owners. I'll be honest, it's more of a love-hate thing. I really hate to sit down and make that first call. The people I call are usually resistant; they don't want to work with agents because they want to sell their houses on their own. But I love the part about knowing that if I can push past that feeling of being uncomfortable, then I will become much stronger when it comes to prospecting. There's nothing that tickles my fancy more than calling a For Sale By Owner who's ready to hang up on me, 20 minutes later getting an appointment, then going to the house, and finally, hours later, leaving with the listing. I just love that! And so will you.

Of all the approaches to prospecting, For Sale By Owners is perhaps the best. Why? Because you know they want to sell. Don't you want quick and "easy" money? Who better to get a listing from than someone who wants to sell? All the other approaches to prospecting can take longer. Despite my recommendations to prospect with FSBOs, you might find that you can't get passionate about calling FSBOs yourself. If you can't, then find another approach you can get excited about.

With that said, let me share with you the 10 key prospecting concepts. You can use these for any type of prospecting that you do.

10 Key Prospecting Concepts

Let's examine some of the thoughts and concepts about prospecting. It's important to look at these concepts first, because you'll find that the thoughts and concepts about a particular topic are sometimes more important than the tips and techniques themselves. Why is that? Because if you really "get" the concept, and you can wrap your brain around it, you'll often come up with your own techniques, because you've got the concept behind the techniques.

Prospecting Concept 1: Prospecting Is the First Link to Success

Visualize a chain. At the end of that chain is a link; let's call that link "money." You got into real estate because you wanted to accomplish something, and, most likely, the more money you make, the better you'll be able to accomplish that thing.

To make more money in real estate, you've got to have more closings, the next link in the chain. In order to have more closings in real estate, you've got to have more contracts, because not all of the contracts that are written actually wind up making it to closing. And how do you get more contracts? You do so by getting more listings. To get more listings, you've got to attend more appointments. And how do you attend more appointments in real estate? You've got to schedule them. In order to schedule them, you've got to prospect.

As you can no doubt tell, the first link in prospecting is the most important. The more prospecting you do, the more listing appointments you're going to schedule. The more appointments you get, the more listings you're going to get. The more listings you get, the more contracts you are going to draw up. The more contracts, the more closings. And the more closings you have, the more successful you are going to be. You will definitely reap financial rewards.

Prospecting Concept 2: Educate Yourself

To better yourself with prospecting, you must keep educating yourself. One area where you have to keep educating yourself is promotion. Constantly look for any new promotional ideas, but be careful about what you spend your money on. I've seen many agents who have "prospected" themselves out of real estate. Here's an example: an agent may hear that "farming"—identifying and cultivating new potential leads (we'll talk about farming in Chapter 8)—is important. So, he gets a list of a number of homes and he'll say to himself, *I'm going to mail these people something every month.* And, of course, being that farming is a numbers game, the more people someone mails, the better return he or she will get. So, that agent may start mailing to a thousand homes each month.

Perhaps the agent attended a seminar, heard about a great promotional item, and bought a package of things to mail to people on his list. Let's say the things to be mailed are refrigerator magnets—you know, the kind that has the company's logo and perhaps the agent's face on it, which the people can hang on their refrigerators. People always need that kind of stuff. So, the agent has the magnets made up. Then he has to create a letter to go with the mailing. Keep in mind: this is *one* mailing, to a thousand people. That one mailing can cost up to a dollar per piece of mail. So, now he's looking at a cost of $1,000 for one month's mailing. Now, multiply that cost by 12 ($1,000 cost per mailing × 12 months), and that gives him a yearly mailing cost of $12,000. If an agent keeps spending that kind of money, he or she will be out of real estate by month 13.

In your effort to get the type of business that you desire, be careful not to invest in the next best thing that you think will be the "magic pill" for success. It doesn't work that way; success takes time.

So, keep educating yourself about ways to promote yourself and continue to invest in promotions, but be smart about what you're spending your money on. And don't just educate yourself about "tricks of the trade" to get your name out there. Invest your time and money in educating yourself about the real estate trade. Attend seminars, take training courses, and go to motivational sessions. Constantly keep feeding your brain; that's the best thing you can do. Any investment that you can make to educate yourself—whether it be time, money, or both—is a good one. You cannot be overtaught. Remember the expression: the more you learn, the more you earn.

Prospecting Concept 3: Find Your Passion

Find the form of prospecting you can get passionate about. I've talked about this in Chapter 2, but the subject bears repeating. That fervor will keep you motivated, focused, and on track.

Prospecting Concept 4: Build Relationships

Build relationships today to make the phone ring tomorrow.

The first way to initiate a relationship is to break down any barriers of resistance that you may find. To illustrate, let's examine a likely scenario where you're trying to build relationships with potential clients over the phone and get them to trust you.

Say that you're calling a For Sale By Owner. Most likely that person will see you as just a salesperson who is trying to take money away from her for your own personal gain. That person is not looking at you as a human being, because she doesn't know you. When you are using the phone to prospect, you don't have the advantage that a face-to-face encounter brings: that one-on-one interaction in person, the personal touch. You need to break down the barriers.

How to do that? Imagine a straight line. At the beginning of that line you have 0 percent, and at the end you have 100 percent. When you have 100 percent it means that you're guaranteed to get in the door. At 0 percent you've got no chance at all. When you call a FSBO, if you try and ask for the appointment within the first 60 seconds, you've got a 0 percent chance of getting that appointment because that person undoubtedly doesn't like or trust you. You need to get the FSBO to stay on the phone with you. The secret to doing that? Ask a lot of questions. When you are engaged in conversation, then you are building a relationship with the other person. The more you do that, the better chances you have for the person to like you. She starts to get the sense that you're not so bad after all. You're not somebody who's out to "get" her. Now, with a dialogue underway, you've got a 50 percent shot of getting in the door.

How to get to 100 percent? If you can get a prospect to like you *and* trust you, it's almost guaranteed that you will get the appointment. And trust can be built by being honest in your dealings with the other person and showing her that you really do have her best interests at heart (namely, a listing—and sale—that's most advantageous to her).

The same thing happens on an actual listing appointment. When you get in the door, the person may not like you at first. If you get her to the point where she trusts you 100 percent, you'll leave with the listing. This concept applies to all methods of prospecting.

Always keep in mind that your job is to build good relationships with a lot of people, just like, say, the mayor of your town does. You need to engage in continual self-promotion. Self-promotion is to have people know your name, your face, and what you do for a living. If people know you, and if they like you and trust you, business will come to you.

One important aspect of building relationships, which applies to all of prospecting, is to always follow up on every lead. You've got to think like a businessperson. Once you start to get names and referrals of people, you need to collect their names, addresses, telephone numbers, and e-mail addresses. You may even get the names and birth dates of their children as well as the names of their pets. Be sure to collect and organization this information well. As I mentioned earlier, it's important to have good file systems so that you can locate this information easily and use it to help you follow up on your leads. The more information you have about people, the better equipped you are to start sending out birthday cards and other items of interest to them. And this information will help you build relationships with them and get them to like you.

My personal experience has taught me what happens when you don't follow up. For example, on some occasions I met people at parties or other social occasions and they expressed an interest in buying or selling real estate. I came real close to getting appointments with them, too. And what happened? I dropped the ball. I forgot to follow up, then I got wrapped up in something else, and I didn't keep good records. I lost the leads to someone else. Irksome? You bet. So, follow up!

Prospecting Concept 5: Everyone Who Owns a House Is a Lead

This concept should get you excited. It involves market analysis of homes.

A market analysis is simply an analysis of how much a person's home is worth on the market at any given point in time. Everybody should conduct an market analysis from time to time, to get an accurate assessment of the status of their investment. Investors with retirement funds do much the same thing with their investments. Periodically, they check up on them to see how they are doing. If the funds are not doing well, then the investors make some corrections and changes. Well, a home is one of your most important long-term assets, isn't it? So, why not find out how it's doing?

I believe everybody should get an updated market analysis on how much their house is worth every two years. Here are two important reasons why.

Number one, homeowners should just know. Every other year, or even every year, people should get a sense of what their net worth is. If the worst thing happened to us and we had to sell everything we own and pay off everything we owe, we would need to know what our net worth is. Most people don't think this way—but they should.

The second reason why all homeowners should reevaluate the value of their homes every other year (or every year) is because, especially in a booming market, most likely they are underinsured. If an owner's house meets with some kind of tragedy, that person may not have enough insurance money to cover the property damage. Unfortunately, this is just what happened to many people in Louisiana and Mississippi whose homes were demolished during Hurricane Katrina and its aftermath in 2005. So many of the homeowners did not have enough insurance to cover the full value of their homes.

Nowadays, insurance policies often have what's called an "escalation clause," which is tied to the cost of living. So, the coverage for the insured goes up each year. But, more times than not, the coverage does not keep up with the appreciation of the property. For example, suppose somebody paid $300,000 for a home eight years ago. With the increase in property values during the real estate boom, the home is now worth $700,000. But the insurance coverage might have increased to cover only $500,000. If the house burned down, that person would lose $200,000. So, you can see why getting the right amount of insurance is crucial.

When you know of people who have not had an updated market analysis on their homes over the past two years, you should propose to them that you come over and give them one. Just ask when was the last time that they had a market analysis on the property for homeowners insurance. For any answer over a year, show your surprise and explain to that they may be underinsured. Then offer to do an informal report of what their house is worth.

Keep in mind: you can't legally do an appraisal of what a property is worth for insurance purposes unless you're a certified appraiser. But the homeowner can take the information you give him and share it with his insurance agent; then the agent can order an official report, if it's warranted.

Does this activity on your part help you get listings? It does; here's how. What's interesting is that most homeowners think their houses are worth less than what the market says they are until they decide to sell; then greed often kicks in and the prices gets inflated beyond what the market will bear.

Long-time homeowners are notorious for nitpicking. They know about all the stuff that doesn't work in their houses. They know that the bushes need to be trimmed, that the ceiling is stained, that the fence needs mending, that the pipes make a lot of noise, and so on. Just like some married couples long after the glow of the honeymoon has worn off, they find flaws and exaggerate every darned thing that annoys the heck out of them. Sometimes they'll focus more on the things that annoy them than on the positives that are still there. With all the haranguing, the homeowners convince themselves that their homes are worth much less than the market value.

So, how can you take advantage of this situation and get listings? Here's how. Imagine that you go to a couple's house and, after previewing the place, you give them the good news: "Your home is worth *a lot* more than you think it is, certainly more than you paid for it." They probably would respond with, "My house is worth that?" You continue with, "You know, based on the equity you have in your property and based on the interest rate you're paying now, there are some other houses that are actually bigger than this house for basically the same monthly payment you're paying now. So, you could actually get more of a house than what you've got right now." See? You can create sellers who weren't even thinking of selling before you went to see them.

Prospecting Concept 6: FSBOs Are the Best Leads

According to a national study, about 70 to 80 percent of all For Sale By Owners wind up listing eventually with an agent. The percentage fluctuates from year to year and from market to market, but it's pretty much in that 70 to 80 percent range. I've seen some markets where almost 90 percent of FSBOs actually wind up listing with an agent. But, let's just figure on the low side: 70 to 80 percent. That means, if in your market you had five new For Sale By Owners selling their houses every month, that's 60 new potential listings each year. If 70 to 80 percent of those sellers wind up listing with an agent and selling, that means 45 to 48 new listings each year. Say that you just got somewhat less than half of those—20—and that 100 percent of these 20 did wind up selling. At a $3,000 commission on each end, that's $60,000 just from the For Sale By Owners. And this is a conservative number! Where I live, we were getting about 20 to 30 new listings a month.

So, for any FSBOs who list, get them to list with *you*.

Prospecting Concept 7: Don't Sweat the Next Step Until You Have Mastered the Previous One

This concept applies to both working the telephones and going on listing appointments. Picture an inexperienced agent sitting across from a seller on a listing appointment, nervous and excited. The agent is trying to focus, but unfortunately he's focused on what he's going to say as soon as that seller stops talking. He's thinking about what comes next, what the next step is, and not what the seller is saying to him. And he gets so uncomfortable in his head that he messes up the whole appointment.

Do not worry about what's coming next, what's around the corner. Just be in the present moment. I've learned something about this recently. I've been dabbling with comedy again, taking improvisation classes in how to make up your own script on the spot, feeding on what the other person tells you and running with that. (You may be familiar with the Drew Carey show *Who's Line Is It Anyway?*, shown on cable TV in reruns, in which this very same thing is done.) One thing I've taken from that class is how important it is to be in the moment.

How I wish I had understood that on my first gig at Caroline's in New York City, a famous comedy club! There I was, getting ready to be introduced and go on, and I start getting nervous. I couldn't remember what I wanted to say after my first joke. I knew my routine, because I had practiced a lot. All I had to do was to remember my first line.

Fortunately, I talked some sense into myself. I just said to myself: *All right, Darryl, you know Step 1. Just trust yourself that Steps 2, 3, 4, and the rest of them will come. Just do Step 1 and watch what happens.* Well, my act was great, I thought. I trusted enough in the moment that the next step just came naturally. So, don't worry about the next step until you've done the previous one.

As I learned in improv class, don't write the whole script in your head either, because you don't know what the other person is going to say. How can you have it in your head what you're going to do five minutes from now? You can't, and you shouldn't, because what the other person says may take you in a totally different direction. Keep that in mind as you go on your listing appointments.

Some basic structure is needed as you go into a listing appointment and calling on a For Sale By Owner, just as in an improv class. You have got to have the basics of who, what, where, when, and why, but then, as the meeting or call is underway, you've got to let go and just go with the flow. Most agents who are not good at prospecting or on listing appointments are that way because there are too focused on trying to do things the "right way." There is a distinction between *being* and *doing*. Too many agents are trying to "do" their careers. If you watch a ballerina, a ballerina does not "do" ballet, she "is" ballet. I had one student who said to me, "It's like playing the drums. You can't think, 'What do I do next?' because your mind can't move as quickly as your hands need to move. You have to 'be' the music and just trust that it's going to work."

Markus Wasmeier from Germany won the gold medal in the men's downhill skiing event in the 1980 Winter Olympics at Lake Placid, New York. After he won, the reporter asked him, "How did you feel going into the race?" Markus replied: "The mood for me to win was right. I felt no pressure, no stress. When you think too much, then you're thinking, not skiing. I know I'm losing when all I'm thinking about is the next marker. I know I've done good when I get to the bottom, and all I remember is the top." In other words, what Markus was saying is that when he's thinking about "doing" skiing, he knows he's going to lose, but when he lets himself go and just "is," then all of a sudden he's powerful and he's a gold medal winner. I'm not saying you shouldn't learn what to say when you're calling FSBOs or on listing appointments, but you've got to be willing to throw it all away and just "be" a powerful real estate agent as opposed to "doing" it.

Prospecting Concept 8: Create a Prospecting Schedule

Notice something about people who are really into working out at the gym, three, four, or five times a week? They are addicted to it. They work their lives around the commitment to working out. And if they miss a day or two, they feel out of sorts, they don't feel powerful, they feel lethargic and tired and have a lack of energy. What they have done is created a habit or a routine when it comes to working out.

I feel the same way when it comes to prospecting in my business. If I skip a day of prospecting that I know I wanted to do or I am committed to doing, I feel frustrated and upset with myself. When I was an agent, the same thing was true about prospecting. I called FSBOs Sundays, Mondays, and Tuesdays, and if I missed a day, I felt like I missed a whole week's worth. I felt like I lost thousands of dollars, which I was not happy about. You really want to get to that point, too.

When I started training for the marathon, I had to plan my schedule and routine, and stick to it, just like I did with my prospecting. The first thing I did, before I showered or anything else, was to go for a run, because I knew as soon as I started getting into my other routine, I would distract myself. And do you know what? It worked.

You need to create some kind of prospecting schedule for yourself that you can keep; everything and everybody else needs to work around that schedule. For example, if you're going to do mailings, schedule them for a certain day and at a certain time, and that's your prospecting schedule. Limit your phone calls to only the most essential ones and don't allow yourself to be interrupted. Call it your "power hour of prospecting."

Prospecting Concept 9: Homeowners Will Make More Money Listing with You

You must believe this! Most homeowners who are thinking of selling have the tendency to want to try and do it on their own. They do so because they think they can save having to pay the commission. You have to believe in your heart that homeowners who sell on their own not only are not saving money, they are actually losing it. In fact, most homeowners will make more money working with an agent than they would on their own. If you want to get some really great evidence that proves this, read my other book published by McGraw-Hill, entitled *How to Become a Power Agent in Real Estate.*

One way or another, you've got to find some statistics and evidence to back up your claim that a homeowner will make more money working with you. Then convince the seller that this will happen. You need to be convinced of this yourself so that you can work truthfully and confidently with the seller to get her or him the best deal.

Prospecting Concept 10: Listings Are a Promotional Tool

The reason why prospecting for listings is so important is because the more listings you get, the more your phone is going to ring. As I've said elsewhere, listings are the foundation to a successful real estate career. There's no getting around it. Your success or failure is going to be relative to how many listings you've gotten in a year. Every listing you get is an opportunity for you to place an ad in the paper, which promotes you. You always want to be promoting yourself, and listings are the tools to do that. In the next three chapters you'll find out how to service sellers to get their houses sold, and I'll get into more specifics on how you use listings to promote yourself. But now let's move into a few of my specific ideas on what you can do to start prospecting.

Prospecting Techniques

Prospecting Technique 1: Expand Your Sphere of Influence

The first thing you need to do is make a list of everyone you know and start keeping track of all the people you meet. In real estate this is known as your *sphere of influence*. It's called a sphere of influence because it consists of a circle of people you know, who know other people, who in turn know other people, who know still more people, and so on. What's really great about a sphere of influence is that after you've been working with one for a while, you'll start to get leads from it. You might hear from someone who has decided to do something related to real estate, or perhaps you hear from somebody who knows somebody else who needs to make a real estate transaction. So, you need to make a list of everyone you know and keep track of all the people you meet: friends, family members, doctors, school friends, car mechanics and tradespeople, dentists, lawyers, neighbors, and more. Be sure to go to www.New AgentSuccess.com, where there is a list of "memory joggers"—things to help jog your memory about the types of people you should be tracking.

All of these people know you and, it is hoped, like you. You need to get in touch with these folks on a regular basis, maybe once a quarter, no more. Contact can be by mail or telephone, but you need to keep your name in front of them. This sphere of influence should be people with whom you have some kind of relationship. This is unlike "farming," a concept discussed in detail in Chapter 8, where you deal with people who you don't know at all, who you have no relationship with, and you contact them once a month either by mail or telephone.

So you've made up a list of everyone you know. Be sure to put it in your contact manager so that the information is readily available. The second thing you want to do in prospecting is to announce your new career to this group by sending them the following letter:

Dear Friend,

It's been some time since we've spoken. I have taken a new course in my life. I am happy and excited to say that I have passed the state license exam to be a real estate agent. Now I've done some extensive research to make sure that I aligned myself with the best possible company that can support me and my friends with their real estate needs. I found it here at Power Realty.

I know how important it is in business that we deal with people whom we like and trust. So, I want you to know that if you ever need anything in the area of real estate, I'm here to support you 100 percent.

Also, because this is a new venture for me, I am so excited for my friends and family that I have partnered up with an agent in the office, who has a great deal of experience. Her name is _____, she has been in real estate for _____ years, and her production is _____. I'm very happy and fortunate to be lined up with her.

Of course, if you know of anyone else who is thinking about buying or selling, I ask that you have him or her give me a call.

And then you should close this letter with something that might be personal like *I hope we can get together soon. I hope the family is well.*

Naturally, you should take the letter and personalize it to your style. If you do make changes to the letter, make sure you include that you have researched the real estate companies and you believe this company is the best. Also, let them know that you need their help and that they should contact you if they know anyone who is thinking of moving. You can also offer an updated market analysis:

> If you haven't gotten an appraisal on your current home in the past 12 months, please let me know. I'd be happy to use our computer system that will help determine the current market value of your home.

Maybe even sell it a little bit. Keep in mind, when you let people in your sphere of influence know that you are now in this career, be sure that they are aware that you're new to it. Because of that, they may already like you, but they may not trust that you know everything. That's why it's important you let them know that you've hooked up with a Real Estate Buddy in your office.

It's important that you sell things a certain way. For example, don't sell the market analysis this way:

> If you haven't done an updated market analysis on your property in the past 12 months, please let me know. I'd be happy to do it for you. Even though I'm new in the business, we have a computer system in our office that pulls up the information of all the properties that have sold in the past several months, and that is the basis that helps determine value. I'd be more than happy to share that information with you.

What you're doing here is stressing the power of this technology, this computer system, this software. This approach will lessen the confidence that they should have in you, and perhaps it will increase their concern about you not being sufficiently skilled or experienced.

You could also include with the letter a copy of the newspaper ad your broker bought that announced you joining the company. Such a vote of confidence in you by your broker should be shared with the people you want to impress.

Prospecting Technique 2: Keep a Good Database of Your Sphere of Influence

What always amazes me is people who have been in this business a long time failing to keep a good database. I remember that when I first got into doing real estate seminars, I would encounter experienced speakers who had been in the business a lot longer than I had (as many as 10 or 15 years) who never really kept a good database of their students or people who attended their seminars. It only took me a short period of time to build up a database of about 60,000 people. And did that database come in handy when I needed some new leads, wanted to generate listings, and also wanted promote myself? You bet!

Every business owner will tell you that one of the most valuable things a business has is its client base, its database. It helps a lot in generating business, pure and simple. So, if you don't have some kind of system to track all the leads you will generate, you're at a disadvantage. Make sure when you list members of your sphere of influence that you keep that information in some kind of organized filing system. The preferred format is a contact management database system. But it doesn't matter what system you use; hardcopy files work just as well (although they are cumbersome). Just be sure to do it.

Prospecting Technique 3: Call FSBOs

Callings FSBOs is absolutely the best source of listing leads. If you can master the art of calling For Sale By Owners, you will truly master the whole real estate profession. The next chapter is devoted to this important topic.

These are three of the most essential prospecting techniques. I'll cover additional techniques in the chapters that follow, as they apply to the various types of prospecting.

Tips for Becoming a Master at Prospecting

Here are some additional tips to being a master at prospecting. Learn these, practice them regularly, and make them a part of your daily habits. You'll become a master before you know it.

1. **Pick a day to prospect and stick to it.** Just like the regular gym-goer does with his or her workout schedule, you must establish a schedule for days of the week and times of the day to prospect—and stick to it. Everything else needs to revolve around that schedule. If you try and work prospecting around the rest of your schedule, you will

always have distractions that keep you away from prospecting. Avoid such distractions. Check your voicemail or e-mail later. Delay that phone call home to make sure that everything is okay. Postpone that check-in with a fellow agent about a business matter. You have the power to do this, because you are creating the distractions. It's always easy to find ways to put off things you know you should be doing. Don't let procrastination become a way of life. Concentrate on the business at hand: prospecting.

2. **Seek to get "in the zone."** You must have heard sports commentators refer to a player who is "in the zone." This phrase refers to someone who playing at his or her very best—or even better than his or her very best. This is the level you want to achieve as a prospector. But, you need to get warmed up to get to that point. Whenever I prospect, I know that I will mess up my first few calls because I need to get into zone. Once I start to make a few calls, I get warmed up and become more effective after each and every call. Quite honestly, there is an easier way to "get in the zone." If you follow through on the tips below before you make your calls, you should find yourself performing at, or even above, your peak.

   ■ **Keep reminding yourself why you are doing this.** What is it that you want to accomplish in your life by being successful at real estate? Is it to be financial free and get out of debt? To buy a vacation home? To take care of your family? The clearer you are about what you are committed to, the more passionate you will be during your calls.

   ■ **Review the dialogue and scripts I gave you.** Take a moment to read through the dialogue so you get comfortable with it. When you are talking with someone on the phone, you don't want to be too focused on the script; you need to focus on what that person is saying.

3. **Set a goal as to what you want to accomplish.** Tell yourself, *I will get two listing appointments before I leave the office tonight.* It may seem odd, but when you verbally declare what it is you are going to accomplish, the universe usually supports you in achieving it.

That's it for the basics of prospecting. For the specifics of how to do those all-important For Sale By Owner prospecting calls, move on to the next chapter.

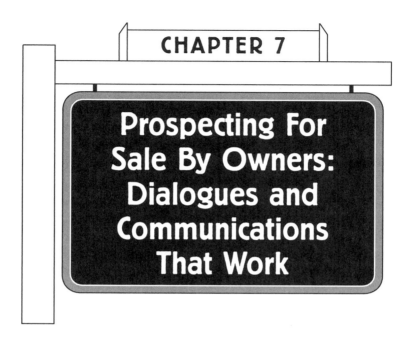

CHAPTER 7

Prospecting For Sale By Owners: Dialogues and Communications That Work

In the previous chapter, I explained how cold calling For Sale By Owner listings can be the key to reaching your goal of a six-figure income. This chapter shows you how. It features my proven, tried-and-true sales dialogues that have helped me achieve great success.

Mastering Calls with For Sale By Owners

Calling and working with FSBOs is my strength. I've found that once you have gotten the concepts and dialogue down, it's easy. So, let me tell you how.

The trick to working with FSBOs is to achieve Three Levels of Mastery. Be sure not to get hung up on using the right techniques, the right scripts, the right dialogue, or whatever. And don't get ahead of yourself and worry about the next level of mastery before mastering the previous one. These are common pitfalls that agents make; avoid them.

Three Levels of Mastery of Working For Sale By Owners

1. **Level 1: Picking Up the Phone and Making Calls.** Level 1 is getting past the fear of picking up the phone in the first place. So, don't worry about getting the appointment later on; focus instead on getting comfortable with the routine of making the calls. The experience, at first, can be a little daunting: the FSBO is not receptive to the call, no one really knows anyone, the timing may not be right, and so on. But, with practice, you can become good at it—and master it.

   And don't be afraid of failure! Remember the story I told you in Chapter 1 about my son Michael and our game of checkers? He would make a scene whenever he lost, but when he finally won and I, the loser, sat there, dumbfounded, he just said, "You learn from your mistakes." What a happy moment. He's right; you do. Learn from Michael.

   People can find it rough going later in life if they don't give themselves permission to mess up. So, practice doing so. You need to be okay with it when you make mistakes because that makes you stronger. You need to have some sort of "breakdown" from time to time, because that enables you to archive a breakthrough. And when you do that, you're that much better equipped to handle whatever situation comes your way. Look at what test pilots in the Air Force do. Their job is to push a plane beyond its limitations because they know that if they do that and they find a breakdown in the machinery of the aircraft, they'll have a breakthrough.

   Think of it this way:

   Breakdown + open-mindedness + corrective action = breakthrough

   In fact, the size of the breakthrough is often equivalent to the size of the breakdown. So, get past your fear and make those calls.

2. **Level 2: Getting the Appointment.** The next step is actually getting the appointment. The section below entitled "General Approaches to Getting the Appointment" discusses in detail how to go about clinching the appointment.

3. **Level 3: Getting the Listing.** Level 3 is mastering actually getting the listing, when you're on that face-to-face appointment. See Chapter 9 for details of what to do when you're on that appointment.

The Importance of Mastering Calls with FSBOs

Here's a great reason why it is so important that you master telephone calls with For Sale by Owners. Let's use an example. Imagine that every house that you sell is worth $3,000 in commission. Let's say that you need to go on five appointments for you to get even one listing. If you average 10 phone calls just to get one appointment, you would need to make 50 telephone calls in order to get your five appointments, to generate that one listing that's going to sell.

Do the math. The bottom line is every time you pick up the phone and talk to a prospective seller or homeowner, that call is worth $60:

$3,000 [commission from the 1 listing]/50 [number of phone calls to generate the 1 listing] = $60 [cost per phone call]

If I were to say to you, "I'm going to pay you $60 to talk to somebody who owns a home to try and generate an appointment to meet with her; will you make the call?" would your answer be "yes"? It should be! That's a good fee for making one phone call. The same rate of return is achieved with you calling FSBOs on the telephone. So, get comfortable with it and good at it. It's definitely worth your while.

Finding Prospective FSBOs

How do you find prospective FSBOs? A great place to start is my Web site, www.NewAgentSuccess.com. There's a link there that will take you to a company that will actually e-mail you names of FSBOs.

Other Web sites will provide you with great updated information and links. Ones I recommend are www.ForSalebyOwner.com, www. FSBO.com, www.SalebyOwner.com, and www.ByOwnerSales. com. You can even search Google for FSBOs.

You could also look for FSBOs in the newspaper of your local town. Check out the listings in the Real Estate section and call the FSBOs you see.

General Approaches to Getting the Appointment: A Dialogue

Follow these steps, throw in your own personal style, and before long you'll be getting those listings too!

The "Hard" Approach to Getting the Appointment

The first approach is the more aggressive one you can try if you think the situation calls for it. It is an effective technique for "getting your foot in the door."

Step 1: Identify Yourself

The first thing you do is identify yourself. Just say this:

Agent: *Hi. I'm calling in reference to the ad in the paper.*

You say this first, not: "Hi, this is Darryl Davis from Power Realty." If you did that, you would hear a definite click of a receiver being slammed down. Or you might hear on the other end:

Person who answers phone: *Hold on a second. . . . Mom, Dad, a Realtor is on the phone for you!*

Distant voice on other end (*emphatically*): *We're not home!*

Instead, just say that you are calling in reference to the ad in the paper. If you are not talking to the decision maker, the person answering the phone will say this:

Person who answers phone: *Hold on, let me get my parents.*

Once you get the decision maker on the phone, then you ask the second question in this step:

Agent: *Is the house still for sale?*

The reason to ask this question before you identify yourself as an agent is because if the homeowner knows you're an agent before you ask that questions, he or she will tell you "No, the house is already sold." The following short exchange will follow next:

Agent: *I'm calling about the house for sale.*

Owner: *Yes?*

Agent: *Is it still available?*

Owner: *Yes.*

Now move to the next step.

Step 2: Introduce Yourself

Keep it short and sweet:

Agent: *Hi, this is Darryl Davis from Power Realty. How are you?*

Step 3: Clarify

You want to clarify if the seller is working with agents or not:

Agent: *The reason I'm calling is to see if you folks are open to working with agents in the sale of your property. Are you?*

The owner will either say "yes" or "no" to that question. If the answer is "yes," you need to clarify the response.

Owner: *Yes, we are working with brokers.*

Agent: *Is it currently listed with a broker?*

Why would you ask that? Because it could be. Sometimes the homeowner is still advertising on his or her own but just listed with a broker. If the reply is "no" when you ask if the property is currently listed, just proceed with the dialogue. However, if the homeowner raises objections, you must respond to them:

Owner: *We are not interested in working with brokers.*

Agent: *So, you are trying to sell it on your own, eh?*

Owner: *Yes.*

Agent: *Is that because you folks want to save the commission?*

Owner: *Yes.*

This will no doubt be the exchange, so now jump into the next step.

Step 4: Find Out What They Are Committed To

The most important part of the dialogue, where most agents freeze up, is asking questions. How many questions should you ask? Ask as many as you need to until you have a good sense of what homeowners are committed to and until you think they are ready to let you come over. I've had some conversations last for over 15 minutes before I got an appointment and some that lasted 60 seconds and then I scheduled the appointment. This is where instinct comes in, and you only get that from making a lot of calls.

When you ask questions of For Sale By Owners, the exchange needs to seem like a dialogue, a conversation, not a presentation. If you ask, "So, where are you folks moving to?" and get a response, "Well, we haven't really decided," you wouldn't then ask, "When do you need to get there by?" Get where? They haven't decided. So you really have to listen to what the owners say, because what they say in response to your question is going to determine the next question and the question after that. So you're really going to piggyback on what the owners are saying, what they feed to you. You really need to pay attention.

As mentioned in the previous chapter, most agents are ineffective on the telephone because they really are more concerned about what they are going to say when the owners stop talking rather than with what the owners are actually saying. You need to focus less on you and more on the owners. That will lead you in the direction you want to go. What the owners are saying, how they are hearing what you're saying, how they are reacting, and everything about them really tells you what you're going to say, what you're going to ask, how you're going to ask it, and so forth. So don't be married to the questions you have prepared.

The following questions are important ones to ask. Keep in mind that you don't need to ask all of them. This list just gives you an idea of some of the questions. It will help to jar your thinking.

- Where you folks moving to?
- When do you need to get there by?
  (Or, "What time frame are you working with?")
- Have you seen any houses there yet, or are you waiting for something to happen on this property first?
- What do you like best about the place where you're moving?
- What type of house are you moving to? Is it smaller or larger than your current home?
- The new home sounds lovely. Why did you choose that area to move to?

- How's the activity been on your current property?
  (And the homeowner will usually tell you, "Wonderful, great, we don't need you.")
- How long have you been living in this current house?
- What would happen if you didn't sell this house?
  (This is a great question, because the answer will tell you how committed the homeowner is to moving.)
- What do you like best about your current house?
- Do you have any family over where you're moving to?
- What is the biggest challenge you're finding right now in selling your home?
  (This is a risky question, because sometimes you won't get an honest answer. the owner will say, "We're not having any challenges." Try to establish some rapport and trust to get a reliable response.)
- Have you been getting any feedback from the buyers who have come through to see your house?
  (This is a great question, because usually no feedback is given, which will create some anxiety for the homeowner. And if feedback is given, the buyers usually say, "We love it. We'll get back to you." And then they never do.)
- Have any of the buyers that have come through made an offer yet?
- Have you ever worked with an agent before in selling a house?
- The house that you purchased, did you do that privately or through an agent?
  (This is a great question, because normally the homeowner will respond, "Oh, we bought through an agent." And isn't that ironic? They bought through an agent but didn't think it worthwhile to sell through one, to save money on the commission. But don't address that particular irony.)

When you're asking these questions of homeowners, take care not to start handling any objections or getting into too much detail. This step is just for you to gather information. If you start doing a listing appointment on the telephone with them, they are going to get defensive. Your main objective when you call For Sale By Owners is to see if you can help them and to get in the door.

Step 5: Invite Action

Another way to say "invite action" might be "close." But I like the phrase "invite action," because here you're going with the consultative approach, not the manipulative way of selling. In this step, you are inviting homeowners to take action based on what they are committed to. Remind them that if they are committed to selling, *all* options should be explored—which includes meeting you.

You have a few ways of inviting action. For instance, you could ask any of the following questions:

- Would you be offended if I just stopped by to see your house? (What is that person going to say? "Yes, I would be thoroughly offended!" This line works well with expireds.)
- If I can help you move to Central City [or wherever], and you wouldn't have to pay a brokerage fee out of the monies that you need in order to make this move a success, would that be of interest to you?

  (This is a great question to ask a For Sale By Owner after you find out what he or she is committed to. Here's why: This dialogue *sounds* like you are working for free, but really it says the homeowner "wouldn't have to pay a brokerage fee out of the monies that [he or she] *needs*," not "the monies [he or she] wants." What the homeowner wants and what he or she needs are two different things. If the homowner presses you, you should have a prepared response:

Owner: *How can you do that?*

Agent: *Are you familiar with how a buyer agency works and that the buyer may elect to pay us? That is just one example of how that could work, but first let me come over, see what you have, and see if I can help you. If I can't, I will tell you in the first five minutes, so I don't waste your time. Does that sound fair?*)

or

- May I just come over and see the house? I just want to see what I can do to help you.

(Asking this question requires you to be a little more aggressive. You need to be careful when asking this. Why? You don't want to create the impression that you have a buyer for the house and want to come by just to show the property and possibly sell it. Even if you do have a buyer lined up, you don't want to state that. Your objective is to come over and see if you can help the homeowner, pure and simple.)

or

● Mrs. Jones, you are letting complete strangers into your home. Which is real interesting, because you don't really know them or whether they are, in fact, buyers. I think it's brave of you to put yourself in a position like this. Of everybody you let in, I'm perhaps the safest appointment you can give. Why? Because I am licensed by the state to help people get their property sold. Plus, I may have two, three, or maybe five potential buyers. By letting me in, it's like letting in five buyers. You've got nothing to lose and everything to gain. And, once again, I'm not going to convince you to do anything you don't want to. I just want to see your house and see if I can help you. Look at me as just another buyer, okay?

(The point here is the homeowner has nothing to lose and everything to gain. You just want to see the house. That's the bottom line. You could also point out that you are committed to the same thing:

Agent: *As an agent, I'm committed to the exact same thing you are, which is to help sell your home and get you to Florida but for the highest possible price, not for the lowest. So, again, you've got nothing to lose and so much to gain.)*

or

● If I paid you $10,000 to see me, would you do it? (This is a bold statement—and a great way of getting in the door. The response and explanation could go like this:

Owner: *What are you talking about?*

Agent: *Well, I may be able to put an extra $10,000 in your pocket if you let me come over and see your house. And there are a few different ways I can do that. First of all, you may be asking too little for* *your home. There may be some other features and benefits about the property that are not getting conveyed to the buyers, which could cost you in the negotiating process. Also, I may have a buyer who's willing to pay you more than what you're hoping for or asking for now. There are a lot of reasons. The bottom line is, I may be able to put more money in your pocket if you let me come in than if you don't. Here's what's guaranteed: if you don't let me come in, nothing will be different than what you've already got.)*

or

- Mr. Hernandez, I know if you were sick you probably would go see a doctor, and you probably have an accountant do your taxes. If somebody threatened to sue you, you probably would call your attorney. Here I am, I'm a professional just like a doctor, accountant, or lawyer, but my focus is real estate. Now, what's real interesting is, yes, you can sell your own home just like you could do your own taxes, medicate yourself if you were sick, and even represent yourself in court, but the question is, should you? I'm not saying I want you to list with me, but at least let me come over, see your house, see what you have, and see what I can do to help you. At least have a conversation with me. It never hurts to talk to somebody, because the worst that will happen is that we will both leave our meeting more educated about the other. I'll leave more educated about your house and what you have to offer, and that might result in something good for you. And I suggest that you may leave a little more educated, because I have a license from the state, which took over 45 hours to obtain, that says I know what's needed to sell a house. As you've got nothing to lose and everything to gain, let's meet, okay?
  (What's to argue with this? You've explained the reasons logically. The homeowner should willingly invite you in.)

You need to get really good at getting your foot in the door on a For Sale By Owner. One way to do that is to read this section over and over and follow these suggestions. Another way is by doing it a lot. The more calls you make, the more you put yourself out there, the more you give yourself permission to mess up, and the stronger you will become. The more mistakes you make, the stronger you become on the telephone.

The "Soft" Approach to Getting the Appointment: The For Sale By Owner Value Call

Unlike the suggestions in the previous section, which are designed to aggressively get you the appointment, this approach is a little softer.

What you are going to do is call For Sale By Owners, not for the purpose of scheduling the appointment, but to offer something of value: brochures, pamphlets, newsletters, and other informative readings that are designed to help them sell their home. Once you mail them this information and they have read it and educated themselves them about what's involved with the sale, eventually they will start to see how complicated it is to sell their property. At the same time, they will discover how educated real estate agents are. The goal is to get FSBOs to reach the logical conclusion that it would be simpler and better for you to help them with the sale of their home.

Keep in mind that there are two parts to getting a home sold. One is marketing, to generate the buyer activity on a particular property. The second is, after you find a buyer who wants to buy it, making sure the transaction makes it to closing. Most For Sale By Owners don't think about the second part, just the first. You need to stress that this area is one in which they could get into trouble and you're just the person to help them out. How? By emphasizing your role as *director*.

One of the techniques I teach in my live training programs is called the *director's technique*. It's a great technique to use when a homeowner tries to blow you off by saying, "My attorney can help me." This technique involves acting like a director of a large-scale project such as a live theater show. If you've ever seen how one of these shows is put together, you know that a lot of people are involved in the process: a set designer, lighting designer, props person, makeup person, stage manager, and the like. Order is maintained and progress is made by all of these people talking to only one person: the director. He's the ultimate arbiter, communicator, and decision maker. Without the director, the show doesn't go on.

A real estate transaction involves much the same process; participating are buyers, sellers, seller's attorney, buyer's attorney, termite company, engineer company, and the bank. The seller's attorney never talks to the termite company. She never talks to the home inspector that represents the buyers. She never talks to the bank representative. The seller's attorney is not talking to a whole bunch of people—and they aren't talking with her. But all these people will talk to a real estate agent! So an agent is like the glue that keeps a transaction together.

Here's what you say on the value call to make your points known:

Agent: *Hi, I'm calling about your house for sale; is it still available?*

Owner: *Yes, it is.*

Agent: *Ah. This is Darryl Davis from Power Realty, how are you?*

Owner: *Fine.*

Agent: *The reason I was calling is that I noticed your ad in the paper, and I was wondering if you're working with a broker who is going to sell your property?*

Owner: *No, we're not.*

Agent: *Well, that's fine. The main reason for my call is that my company currently has a free report entitled "The 11 Ways to Sell Your House for the Highest Possible Price." I wanted to send this report to you, given that you are trying to sell the house yourself. Now, there's no obligation. The reason I want to send this to you is I'm sure a lot of agents have been calling you and asking to see your house. And some agents probably called because they want to list your home. But here at Power Realty we just want to let you know that we're here to provide a service to you. We want you to know that if you ever do need anything, that we're here to support you. So would you like me to send you this information?*

This simple conversation should get the ball rolling. When the homeowner says "yes," be sure to send the information right away—and follow up within the week. Be proactive!

Another Approach: Knocking on Doors

Some agents (not me) love knocking on doors because they feel they can be much more effective with sellers if they can see the people face-to-face. There's a lot to be said for this technique. Some benefits are that it's easy for agents to build rapport with sellers and it's hard for sellers to be unpleasant when they put a face to the voice. The drawback is that this technique takes longer than cold calling on the phone. But you may get better results with door knocking than with cold calling, so do whatever is comfortable—and successful—for you.

Here's a typical interchange between a homeowner and an agent who's knocking on doors:

Agent *(after knocking): Hi, ma'am. The reason I stopped by is I noticed the sign on the lawn out front [or "I saw your ad in the paper"], and I just wanted to introduce myself. My name is Darryl Davis, and I'm a real estate agent in the area. I'm sure you have probably been getting some calls or agents stopping by.*

Owner *(laughing): Yes. We get more agents stopping by or calling us than we do buyers.*

Agent: *Well, that's the kind of market that we're in. A lot of agents are in the industry, and unfortunately, as you can see, some of them are pretty aggressive. So, how has the activity been on your property? How's everything going?*

After she's told you about what's been happening with the sale of the property, you should start to build rapport with the her. Ask her a bunch of questions about where she's moving to, how long she's been in residence, how long the home has been on the market, and other things that you would ordinarily ask on a telephone call. When you feel like you've built some rapport and trust, then you'll need to ask her the million-dollar question:

Agent: *So, Mary [at this point, we're on a first-name basis], while I'm here, would you be offended if I took a look at your house? May I come in?*

Don't ask this question too soon, or she'll blow you off. But if you have been asking questions and building good rapport, there's a good chance she will let you in. But let's say she doesn't; here's how you should handle that:

Owner: *I'm sorry. I can't let you in. Now is not really a good time.*

Agent: *The reason I ask is because I may have one or two buyers who are interested in your property. By letting me in, it would be like letting in two or three buyers.*

Owner: *Well, now is really not a good time, because I'm running out the door. Maybe you and I could make it for another time.*

Agent: *That's fair. I'd be more than happy to come back another time; I also have somewhere I need to get to. I could just run through the place real quick; it should just take a minute.*

Keep pushing like this a few times to try to get in the door. After all, the homeowner may not be completely honest about having to go somewhere or something to do, so persistence might pay off. I would try up to three times after a negative response from the owner, and, after that, I would leave it alone. But it never hurts to try! Once you're in and touring the home, you might find that the owner opens up, gives you more information, and perhaps even commits to a listing with you.

Follow-up with For Sale By Owners

You already know that follow-up is key to success in getting listings with For Sale By Owners. So here are a few things you can do to stay in touch and to follow up with them. I'm assuming that you have called the FSBOs and haven't gotten in the door, or you did see them but have yet to get their listings.

Thank-You Notes

Write thank-you notes ahead of time. Keep the thank-you notes short and sweet; for example:

> Dear Mr. Cheng,
>
> I really enjoyed our conversation today. I hope that I can be of some service to you in the future. In the meantime, if you need anything or have any questions, please feel free to contact me. My contact information is shown below [and supply the info!].
>
> Sincerely,
>
> Darryl Davis

That's it. It's very simple. I'd have a lot of those written ahead of time, because when you're calling For Sale By Owners, you don't want to make a call, stop, write a letter, make another call, write a letter, stop, write a letter, and so on. When you're making your calls, you want to go nonstop. Then, at the end of the day, you can mail out a notecard to each of the people you have called on. If you're going to pass these homeowners on the way home, another option is to just drop notes in their mailboxes rather than mailing them. But be sure to put stamps on the envelopes. That makes it legal.

Mailings

Send to homeowners anything that you think they need to see, ought to know, or would be of interest to them. For example, you could send free reports, which were mentioned earlier. If the interest rates go up or down, let them know this. A checklist for them or for the kids that they could use when moving would be helpful. Tips on how to hold a public open house would come in handy.

One of the things I teach in my live training programs is the "For Sale By Owner First Aid Kit." This was actually created by Tom Hopkins, but I have a different approach to it. You gather all the items that are necessary to complete a real estate transaction. The kit should include such things as mortgage information, mortgage insurance information, title insurance brochures, a net sheet, open house sign-in sheet, a buyer's net sheet, seller's net sheet, disclosure forms, and sample contracts. Then you bombard the homeowners with mailings, putting one item in each mailing as a gift to them showing them what they need in order to sell their homes. This campaign comes across as though you are helping them; at the same time you are showing them there is more to selling a house than putting an ad in the paper. You are also showing them how knowledgeable you are on the subject of selling a house—more versed in the ins and outs than, say, they might be.

Cover Letters with Mailings

You'll need to include cover letters with each of your mailings so that the homeowners know the purpose of the mailing and get your contact information again. Be sure to include, in prominent letterhead, all the information the homeowners need to phone, e-mail, or visit you. Here are some examples of typical cover letters:

Cover Letter 1: Mailing with Security Checklist

> Dear Mr. Jones,
>
> Congratulations on making the commitment to sell your property. I hope, for your sake, that the experience is a brief one. In the process of selling your home, please make sure you keep yourself and your family safe. I've included here a security checklist of things you need to have in place during the selling process so you and your family are not at risk. If I can ever be of any service to you, please give me a call.
>
> If you want another copy of that security checklist, you can get a copy at www.NewAgentSuccess.com.
>
> Sincerely,
>
> Darryl Davis

Cover Letter 2: Mailing with Seller's Net Sheet

> Dear Ms. Sanchez,
>
> How much you sell your house for is not nearly as important as how much you net. So I've enclosed for you a seller's net sheet to help you figure out exactly how much you should be netting in the sale of your property. If you have any questions about the actual formula, please feel free to give me a call.
>
> Sincerely,
>
> Darryl Davis

Cover Letter 3: Mailing with Free Report

> Dear Mr. Bhatti,
>
> Selling your house can be a challenging experience. My personal experience has told me that there are some mistakes that home-owners make that can cost them thousands of dollars. Therefore, I've included a free report to help you avoid some of the common mistakes homeowners have made in the past when selling their own homes.
>
> Sincerely,
>
> Darryl Davis

Follow-up with the Mailings

Follow up is crucial; you want to do it regularly and often. First, you should call the people and try and get in the door. If you are unsuccessful doing that, put them into some kind of mailing campaign that you create. Maybe it's a 14-day campaign. It's actually 10 mailings, Monday through Friday. But that doesn't mean you don't keep calling them. So maybe on day 5 you'll do a follow-up call. You'll still want to call and try and get in the door. So if you have been mailing things for at least two weeks, you should have called them at least a couple of times.

A few days after that last mailing, you could do a follow-up call asking them if they've been getting their mailings. I would do this every day for at least 5, 10, or 14 days, and do follow-up calls in between, periodically.

Some Tips for Working Only For Sale By Owner Calls

When to Call FSBOs

When is the best time to call For Sale By Owners? I always prefer to call them Sunday, Monday, and Tuesday evenings after 6:00 p.m. I choose those days because often the owners are frustrated after showing over the weekend to no avail. If no one has shown up or if a lot of people have shown up but no one has made an offer, that would be a letdown. And what better time to call with a pep talk and explanation of why you could produce better results?

Another good reason for these times is that the FSBOs are usually available. If you called just before the weekend or during the weekend, usually they would just ask you to call back after the weekend anyway. So I prefer to call right after the weekend.

To Leave or Not to Leave an Answering Machine Message?

Should you leave a message on an answering machine with FSBOs? My thinking is: it doesn't hurt. If you don't leave a message, you will still call them later on anyway. And if you leave a message and they don't call back, you can call them again in a few days.

The message I would leave for a For Sale By Owner is:

Hi, this is Darryl Davis from XYZ Realty. The reason I'm calling is that I've noticed you are selling your house, and I have some important information. I might even have somebody who might be interested. I need to get some more information. So, please call me back.

You want to try and entice the sellers a little bit to motivate them to call you.

So, now you know how to go about getting the listing appointment with For Sale By Owners, where you should be focusing most (if not all) your efforts. Chapter 9 will show you what to say on the actual listing appointment to clinch the deal. But first, let's examine alternative, non-FSBO types of prospecting, the subject of our next chapter.

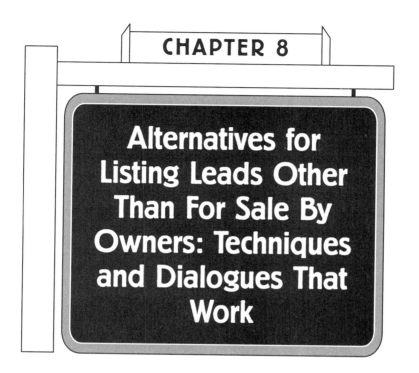

CHAPTER 8

Alternatives for Listing Leads Other Than For Sale By Owners: Techniques and Dialogues That Work

You now know how to prospect for For Sale By Owners and have become familiar with dialogues you can use to get the listing appointment. You should be focusing on these all-important FSBOs, for reasons mentioned elsewhere. But you can and, when the occasion calls for it, should do other types of prospecting for listings. This chapter will show you how to do that. You'll also see some dialogues you can use to make your prospecting efforts successful.

Expired Listings

Expired listings involve people who tried to sell their homes at one point, listed their properties with a real estate agent on the Multiple Listing Service, failed to sell their properties, and then no longer listed with their original broker of choice. There are two great things about expireds. First, you know they want to sell, and second, they are not opposed to working with real estate agents—or at least they weren't when they first signed with another agent.

The first thing you need to do is to get a list of expireds. Even though expireds listed with the MLS and did not sell, their information should still be on your MLS. All you have to do is print out all the homes that expired, let's say in the past 30 days, and then you have your list. Some MLSs give you the ability to print out the list of homes that are *going to* expire. This is an awesome capability, and if your MLS has that function you should use it; just print out your list ahead of time and mark your calendar to call each expired listing the day it expires. Don't call before the listing expires, because that would be a violation of your license law.

You should also pay close attention to the MLS three times a month. Here's why: most agents, when they list a house for sale, usually round off the expiration date to the first, fifteenth, or last day of the month. So for example, if they want to do a six-month listing, and it's now January 5, they may have the listing expire on June 15 or June 30. It could even be July 1. So, make sure you check the MLS on those days of the month.

To be most effective, you really need to check the MLS every day. Just go to the MLS each morning, and print out all the houses that expired in the last 24 hours. Someone in your office can do this; find out from somebody in your office how to use your MLS most effectively for you.

How do you get the information about the expireds so that you can call them? There are a couple of ways. From the listing itself, you have the address and the name of the homeowner; you can usually access the phone number from public records, from the reverse directory, or from the telephone book.

Expired Listing Dialogue

The dialogue you would have for an expired listing would be similar to that for the For Sale By Owner.

Step 1: Identify

Agent: *Hello, may I speak with Mr. Jones?*

Owner: *This is he.*

Step 2: Introduce

Agent: *This is Darryl Davis from Power Realty, how are you?*

Owner: *Fine.*

Step 3: Clarify

Agent: *The reason I am calling is that I noticed your house expired off the Multiple Listing Service and I was wondering if the house is still for sale.*

Owner: *Yes, the house is still for sale.*

Agent: *Have you put it back on the Multiple Listing Service?*

Owner: *No.*

If the homeowner has given this response and the house is still for sale, you now would know that this is a For Sale By Owner.

But let me clarify further. Suppose the homeowner indicates that the house is not for sale. Does that mean that it's off the market? You need to know this, so you need to ask some direct questions. For example:

Owner: *No, the house is not for sale.*

Agent: *Did you sell it?*

Owner: *Yes.*

Seller: *Is it in contract?*

You would ask this last question because the seller might have a buyer who is interested but nothing has been signed yet.

If the property has sold, close the call politely and move on to the next call. If the property hasn't sold, you are ready for the next step in getting the listing.

Step 4: Find Out What They Are Committed To

Agent: *I am looking at a copy of your listing on the Multiple Listing Service, and I am little surprised that the property didn't sell. Why do you think that is?*

Owner: *Who knows? We had a lot of people come through to check on the place, and they expressed interest, but then it died down. And they were very enthusiastic at first. My wife thought it might have something to do with the amount of light this place gets; it's kind of dark. But I don't think that's it at all. I'm baffled. And more than a little frustrated.*

You are likely to hear any one of a number of answers. Maybe the agent didn't do what she was supposed to do. Maybe the weather didn't cooperate; the snow (or rain or whatever) kept people away.

Maybe there were a lot of other homes in the area for sale, which took away potential buyers from the homeowners' place. No matter what answer the homeowner gives, you are likely to hear frustration expressed. Let the homeowner vent.

What happens to cause homeowners to reach this level of frustration? Keep in mind that there usually is a next level that homeowners want to reach. Perhaps they want to get a bigger—or smaller—home. Perhaps they want to move to a nicer or different neighborhood or even state. Perhaps they need to relocate because of a new job. In any case, they are usually very excited about their future. So, a lot of potential buyers come through the house, or not—and nothing happens. After weeks of this inactivity, most owners will take this situation quite personally. And so they get frustrated, upset, and discouraged. Eventually, they just throw their hands up and say, "The heck with it. We're not going to move."

This is a common situation with most expireds. Your job when you're calling expireds is to bring them back that original excitement, that enthusiasm, that next level, the thing that they are very much committed to accomplishing.

You do that by asking several more questions:

Agent: *Why are you folks moving? . . . Where are you moving to? . . . When do you want to get there?*

Find out what they are committed to and bring them back into the presence of why they are selling.

Step 5: Invite Action
At this point, you are ready to initiate action:

Agent: *Mr. Jones, I understand this is probably frustrating for you, but let me ask you this. If I had a buyer who was willing to pay the price that you need to make this move a success, and we can still get you to Florida in the time frame you want and with the money that you need, is that something you'd be interested in? Would you at least consider it?*

Owner: *Yes.*

Most of the time you can breathe life into the process and reinvigorate the excitement and commitment the homeowners had when they first decided to sell their home.

Sometimes, homeowners might not be discouraged and might still be interested in selling but, for whatever reason, they have allowed the listing to lapse. So, ask them if they would still consider selling:

Agent: *Would you still consider selling?*

Owner: *Yes, we're still interested in selling. I don't know what happened with the agent we had. We had it listed with the agent, and all of a sudden we find out that it expired. The agent lost touch with us.*

So, if they still plan on selling, then you go on to asking the questions, "Where are you folks moving to? When do you want to get there by?" So you still move forward with the same dialogue. There just may be a little different slant on it. You still ask the questions about what they're committed to. If somebody is an expired, and they're not frustrated, they're still committed to selling, but they have decided to go the route of a For Sale By Owner, the dialogue again doesn't change.

That's essentially the expired dialogue. Between For Sale By Owners and expireds, there is plenty of business out there for you. Quite frankly, if you just work these two avenues of business, that alone could put you at making a six-figure income in real estate. I say this because these are the two most valuable areas, because we know something about these people: they want to sell. Studies show at least 70 percent of these homeowners are going to list with an agent, so it might as well be you.

Many agents don't make these calls to For Sale By Owners and expireds because fear controls them. (*What if I don't succeed? How do I handle belligerent people? Suppose they ask me questions I can't answer? What if . . . ?*) But you should—and must—do so to get that high income. I've given you the foundation and the dialogue to use to win with the expired. It will take time and practice to get good at this dialogue. Eventually, you'll start to create your own questions. You'll start to adapt the dialogue to your own style, which is what you ought to do.

Orphans

"Orphans" did business with an agent in your real estate office who is no longer working there. You should see if there are still viable business arrangements to be had with these people. First, go to your broker or manager and ask if you can start working the closed transactions—the ones associated with an agent who has left the company. Explain carefully what you propose to do and why, and the broker-manager should release the names and numbers to you.

(Note: Take care not to refer to these people as "orphans." This is real estate lingo I like to use, and think you should as well. But others in your office and, most particularly, the "orphans" themselves, may not understand what you are talking about—and may take offense.)

Here is a simple process you can use to work these orphans.

First, make sure that you have some kind of file system or contact management software. One of the most popular software productions for our industry is called Top Producer, which most people I know love working with. The important thing is to set up some way to easily track these names and numbers.

The second thing that you may do is write a letter introducing yourself. This is one of the letters we give agents in our training program:

> Dear Mr. Jones.
>
> I'm writing this letter on behalf of my company to apologize. You had bought a house through our company five years ago for $180,000 [or whatever the figure is], and it seems that we have lost touch with you. So now I've been appointed as the representative for my company for your concerns; if you ever need anything in the area of real estate, don't hesitate to call me.
>
> Please keep in mind: we are also offering an updated market analysis to past home clients. As you know, one of the most important assets a homeowner has is his or her home, and as with any asset in one's personal life, the owner periodically should get a value of what it is worth in today's market. So, if you would like to get an updated market analysis at no charge, with no obligation, please let me know.
>
> It's a very simple process. You may be amazed to find out how much your house is worth in today's market.
>
> Sincerely yours,
>
> Darryl Davis

Another letter you can send is to those people who are paying private mortgage insurance (PMI). You might be able to provide these folks with a valuable service.

Whenever homeowners put down less than 20 percent when they buy a home, they need to pay an additional monthly payment for private mortgage insurance. This mortgage insurance ensures that if the homeowners should default on the loan, the insurance company will pay the mortgage company or the bank what the buyers owe to them on the loan. This coverage is needed because that less-than-20 percent down payment may not be a financially sound investment, and the homeowners my subsequently default on the loan.

PMI can be gotten rid of when either of two things happens: when the homeowners have paid down enough of the principal so that the value of the home and the principal is greater than that 80-20 spread, or when the home has appreciated in value.

Here's another reason to urge the homeowners to let you provide an updated market analysis: the homeowners can find out whether their home is worth 20 percent or more of what their loan is. And if it is, then they can actually ask the bank to take away the PMI payment. So, you can help the homeowners save money. And how does doing so help you get business? When you provide these orphans with this customer service, the goodwill you establish should make them willing to remain a part of your client base, likely to refer other sellers to you, and likely to list with you in the future, should they decide to sell again.

The information you get from your broker or manager on these closed files should tell you the amount of the loan these people received and the price for which they purchased the home. And you should be able to tell whether they took out a loan for more than 80 percent of the purchase price. If they did, and enough time has lapsed for these people to have paid off a substantial portion of their principal, they may be good candidates to have the PMI removed. Here's a sample of the letter I send out to orphans:

Dear Mr. Jones,

If you have owned your home for more than two years, here is a tip that might save you thousands of dollars. Homes purchased with a loan greater than 80 percent require private mortgage insurance, or PMI. The premium is typically 1 to 2 percent of the mortgage at closing, and approximately $1/4$ to $1/2$ percent per month for the renewals.

When your equity has increased to 20 percent, in most cases you are no longer required to have the PMI, but you will have to petition the mortgage servicer to have it removed. One way for your equity to increase is to reduce the principal down to 80 percent of the original purchase price. However, this reduction usually takes 12 years or more, unless you are making additional contributions to principal.

The most common way for your equity to increase is for the value of your property to increase. The difference between the unpaid balance and what your property is worth is your equity. The mortgage company may require a new appraisal to prove the current worth, but before you spend the money, ask them if they'll accept the assessed value.

Just give me a call at 201-555-6000 and I'll supply you with the assessed values and sales of comparable homes in your area. If there is anything else I can do for you, please let me know.

Sincerely yours,

Darryl Davis

After you have mailed the letter, wait about a week and call the homeowners. Here's the follow-up dialogue that you should use:

Agent: *Hi, this is Darryl Davis from Power Realty. How are you?*
Owner: *Fine.*
Agent: *Good. The reason for the call is to apologize.*

Owner: *For what?*

Agent: *Well, it seems as though you bought a house from our company three years ago. The agent who was involved with that sale is no longer working with our company, and we noticed that we have lost touch with you. I've been appointed as the agent from my office to get in touch with you, introduce myself, and let you know that if you ever need anything related to real estate, I'm here for you.*

Owner: *Well, that's pretty nice.*

Agent: *As a matter of fact, I did send a letter to you in reference to this matter. I don't know if you recall getting it.*

Owner: *I did get the letter, but I get a lot of junk mail. Honestly, I threw it away.*

Agent: *Okay. Well let me ask you, how are things going?*

Owner: *Oh, great, fine.*

Agent: *So, you've been in the house three years. How are you enjoying it?*

Owner: *It's lovely. We're very happy.*

Agent: *Have you made any improvements to the property yet?*

Owner: *No, no. We love it just the way it is.*

Agent: *Okay, great. And what do you like best about the neighborhood?*

Continue to ask rapport-building questions. Then toward the end of the conversation, ask this:

Agent: *I'm curious, do you have an idea how much your house is worth in today's market?*

Owner: *No. Three years ago we paid $400,000 for it. I'm assuming it's worth not too much more than that.*

Agent: *Well, at Power Realty we think homeowners should do an updated market analysis once every two years. It's been three years for you. Your house may have appreciated considerably, and it might be a good thing for me to do an updated market analysis. There are a couple of reasons why I should do so. One of the main reasons is some homeowners have discovered they have actually been underinsured on their property. Sometimes properties have appreciated greater than the* *value the escalation clause in their homeowners insurance policy says it is. So, we feel it's smart business to get an updated market analysis, and it's really a good idea, because it doesn't cost anything. I'd be happy to do that market analysis for you, if you would like me to.*

Now, why would anyone be doing free comparable market analyses for past clients and orphans other than it being a nice customer service thing to do? Because if the real estate market has been hot, as it has in many places the last few years, a lot of homeowners who bought their homes a few years ago might think their house is worth is much less than what it actually is. Here's their thinking process:

Owner: *When I first bought my house, I was excited. I thought it was great. After living here five years, all of a sudden I see all the little things that are annoying me—these minor improvements that I want to make and that we haven't gotten to.*

What they think their house is worth is less than what a buyer coming in fresh might perceive it to be. So, if you do this updated market analysis at no charge to a past client, to an orphan, or to anybody for that matter, all of a sudden they might say, "Boy I didn't realize my house was worth this much." They may decide to put their property on the market because they didn't realize how much equity they had in it—and they may decide to list with you.

Become familiar with this approach to orphans. You'll discover that there's a lot of business in your office in those closed files.

Calling Around New Listings

Any time a house comes up for sale with your company, even if it's not your listing, you can either knock on doors of other houses in the neighborhood or you can "call around" that particular listing. One of the techniques you can use is the 10-10-20 Rule. This technique says that when a new listing comes out on the market, you should knock on 10 doors to the left of that home, 10 doors to the right, and then 20 across the street. The reason you would do so is that people in the homes in the same neighborhood as the listing are likely to know the sellers personally and be willing to help them find a buyer.

Let me clarify: You shouldn't be looking for buyers. That's what your dialogue will sound like, like you're looking for buyers to buy this property. But you should be focusing, as always, on listings.

Here's the call-around approach you should use:

Agent: *Hi, this is Darryl Davis from Power Realty. How are you? I don't know if you're aware of this, but one of your neighbors has recently hired us to sell their home. The reason for the call [or stopping by] is that I thought you should be aware of what's going on in your neighborhood. It's a lovely home. Let me ask you, do you know of anyone who's looking to buy in the neighborhood?*

We do expect a lot of buyer activity from this particular house. So we'll have many buyers who, even if they are not interested in this particular home, will be interested in buying in the neighborhood. Do you know of anyone else who might be contemplating making a move themselves? Let me ask you this: when was the last time you had a market analysis done on your property? Here's why I ask . . .

And then you can go on to explain why it's important to get an updated market analysis.

The "I Have Buyers" Call

This approach can be used on the telephone or with door knocking. It's a good way to help you find some listing leads. But first be sure you actually have people who are interested in buying in that particular neighborhood.

Here's the dialogue for this type of call:

Agent: *Hi, this is Darryl Davis with Power Realty. The reason for this call [or for me stopping by] is that I was wondering if you can help me out for a moment. You see, I'm working with a family that is relocating from San Diego and they have chosen two communities to possibly live in, this being one of them. The problem that we're faced with is that there is very little on the market right now. So I was wondering, have you heard of anyone in the area who's thinking of selling their home?*

Owner: *Gee, I'd have to think . . . The Hidalgos down the street said that they'd like to move to the East Coast within the next year . . .*

Agent: *By the way, have you folks ever thought of making a move?*

Owner: *No, we haven't.*

Agent: *Well, let me ask you this. When was the last time you folks had a market analysis done for your homeowners insurance policy?*

The "Just Sold" Call

You might be able to drum up some listings with this approach, which can be used when calling on the phone or knocking on doors. But, again, as with the "I have buyers" call, make sure that you actually have buyers before you initiate the call. The dialogue should go like this:

> **Agent:** *Hi, my name is Darryl Davis, and I'm with Power Realty. The reason for the call [or for stopping by] is I thought you would like to know that we just sold one of your neighbor's homes. Because that house was for sale, it generated a lot of buyer activity in the neighborhood, and we now find ourselves with a lot of buyers who are interested in the neighborhood and very few homes for them. I wanted to know if you knew of anyone in the neighborhood who is thinking about selling their home. This would be the best time for someone to sell or consider selling.*
>
> **Owner:** *No, I don't really know of anyone at the moment . . .*
>
> **Agent:** *Well, let me ask you this, when was the last time you had a market analysis done on your home?*

The Community Study

This study is designed to find out what your community needs that it currently doesn't have in the way of stores, shops, homes, and parks. Actually, it's a survey to find out what can be done to improve the community. By simply calling a lot of people in a specific neighborhood asking a series of questions about improvements they might like to see in the community, you may flush out somebody who is thinking about selling his or her home. Let me share with you what this type of call may sound like:

> **Agent:** *Hi, this is Darryl Davis from Power Realty. How are you?*

Owner: *Fine.*

Agent: *The reason I'm calling is we're doing a survey of the neighborhood to find out the strengths and weaknesses of the neighborhood, and I would certainly appreciate it if you had about 60 seconds for me to ask you just a handful of questions. When the study is completed, we're going to share the information with everyone who helped us compile the information. So do you have about 60 seconds for me?*

Owner: *Yes. Why, sure, that would be fine. Ask away . . . (This is the answer you'll get about 50 percent of the time.)*

Agent: *What do you like best about the neighborhood? . . . Do you currently have children going to the schools? . . . Do they go to public school or do they attend a private school? . . . What do you like best about the school? . . . What do you think about the community amenities, as far as the stores and shops? . . . What shops or businesses do you think the community needs? . . . If you were to move, would you stay in the state or move out of the state? . . . When was the last time you had a market analysis done on your home for your homeowners insurance policy?*

Take care to ask very brief, very simple questions that are all designed to help flush out some listings.

The Public Open House

A public open house gives the general public the opportunity to tour a home without scheduling an appointment. Of course, you already need to have a listing—or know someone in your office who has a listing and who will let you have the public come look at the property—to hold an open house. But it's a great way to generate listings.

Here's how it usually works. You pick a time frame to conduct the open house, say from 12 to 2. I find that two hours works the best; any more time than that is just overkill. And if you limit yourself to the two-hour time frame, you leave yourself with the opportunity to conduct two or three open houses in one day.

To generate interest in the event, place an ad in the paper saying that you're holding this house open to the general public. Put up signs in the neighborhood. Leave circulars at the local grocery store. Promote the heck out of it. Also, be sure to have balloons and signs on the property on the day of the open house so that people who are driving by know about the showing. Check with your office on the many ways to promote the open house; undoubtedly they have models in place for doing so that work well in the market you are servicing.

In terms of promotion, there are a couple of dos and don'ts. One of the things you want to do is put out as many signs as you possibly can. Most agents only put a sign in front of their property, and at best, one on the corner where the property is located. If you've ever seen a yard sale, what do they do? Do they put out one sign? No. You usually see five, six, even seven signs. They put them on telephone poles and on trees. Most likely the market that you work in says that you can't do that, but many people do it anyway. At the very least, you need to put up as many signs advertising the open house in as many heavily trafficked areas as you can think of. And be sure to take down all your signs when the open house is over!

If you put out a minimum of 10 signs, that will drive a lot of traffic to your open house. That was the policy of the office I used to manage: an agent had to put out a minimum of 10 directional signs per open house. Let me give you an idea of what the signs should look like.

The signs should be the size of flipchart paper but be on hard posterboard material. You should write "Open House" in big, black letters and draw a fluorescent colored arrow that is very big. Be sure to include the address of the open house on the sign. You should then hang the sign up high so that it can be seen from as far away as possible. And hang a sign on every other block, starting from far away and going up to the block of the open house, so you draw people in. It's a very powerful technique.

Most agents are lucky if they get a half a dozen people to attend an open house. The reason is that they usually count on just the advertising in the newspaper. You've got to hope that somebody sees the ad and then schedules his or her day around getting to the open house. That technique is insufficient. But if you are putting out a lot of these signs on a major road, you can get 20 to 30 couples to show up. The bottom line in terms of what to do about promotion is to do what people do for garage and yard sales.

Another thing you want to do with public open houses is to have some kind of sign-in form for the people looking at the house to fill out. Your company should have a form for you to use. But if it doesn't, create your own. The purpose of this form is to have contact information about every prospective buyer on hand; that's where you can get future listings. So have some fill-in-the-blanks on the form for name, address, e-mail address, phone number, and possibly how they heard about the open house, what kind of house they are looking for, and how long they have been looking—and why. The prospective buyers will fill out these sheets with their contact information when they arrive. Sometimes they don't give you real information, but that's just the nature of the beast.

After they sign the form, the best thing to do is let them go through the house on their own. Don't follow them around, because they may feel intimidated. Instead, just tell them, "Feel free to go through. Here's my card. If you have any questions, holler. I'd be more than happy to take you through." In fact, it's even better to ask them, "Would you like me to take you through, or would you like to just go through on your own?" Most of the time they will say they would like to go through by themselves, but by asking them, you won't look like you don't care or can't be bothered.

Before people start coming to the open house, make sure you turn on all the lights. Think like a car dealer. Most car dealerships are very nice, and they use special lights that you often find in a jewelry store. It makes the paint on the cars look like it pops off the frame; it's visually appealing. So do the same thing with the house you are showing. Turn on every single light, even if it's bright outside. When you turn a light on, it's going to make that room brighter, no matter how bright it is outside.

Make sure the place is nasally appealing as well. To get a good smell, use air fresheners or even bake cookies before anybody gets there. Some people even take vanilla extract and put one or two drops on the light bulbs throughout the house.

Make sure you take a tour of the property yourself, before buyers start coming through. Look at the home as the buyers are going to see it.

The last thing you are going to want to do is put together the "open house package." Assemble a little take-away piece. Get some folders and in them place a flyer about the property for sale, company promotional things, a bio sheet about you (along with all contact information), and a checklist for buyers when they are making a move. If you want a copy of the checklist to distribute, go to www.NewAgentSuccess.com.

If you conduct a successful open house, you are bound to generate some interest in the people who are viewing it. And some of them are bound to be potential listings for you, either now or in the future. So, follow my suggestions and have as good an open house as you possibly can.

The Neighborhood Open House

When you conduct a public open house you'll also want to hold a neighborhood open house. If you're going to have a public open house from 12 to 2, invite all the local neighbors to come see the house. But do so by invitation only and hold the event before the public open house. So imagine you have got a public open house from 12 to 2. From 10:30 to 12, by invitation only, the neighbors are invited to take a special, private viewing of the home. You'll find out shortly why this event is so powerful, why you will love doing it, and how it will absolutely generate some listing leads for you.

You will want to create a special flyer, although I prefer that you have something made that looks like a wedding invitation. Either handwrite it or have it designed. And make sure that it looks attractive and professional. Here's what you need to have on this invitation:

> By invitation only, come see your neighbor's house from 10:30 to 12 on March 20 [or whatever the date is]. The homeowners will not be home this day, so they have hired our company to hold an open house so that the general public can view the property. Come before the general public to find out what the homeowner is selling. You never know, you may know somebody who would be interested in buying this property.

What are you telling people here? Number one, you're telling the neighbors that their neighbors are selling their house. Number two, you're letting them know that the sellers are not going to be home. Number three, you're saying, in effect, "Come on, be nosy, and go through their home." What's brilliant about this technique is that you know that those people who come through the house from 10:30 to 12 are not buyers but just neighbors. So you won't be telling them how lovely the home is and focused on trying to sell them the home. And what will you be focused on? Trying to qualify them for a pre-listing conversation.

For this technique to work, you need to go with the neighbors as they make their way throughout the property. Here's what a typical dialogue would be in this situation:

Agent: *So folks, tell me. How long have you lived in the neighborhood"*

Neighbor: *We've lived here about five years.*

Agent: *Really? Great. What do you like best about it?*

Neighbor: *Well, the schools are great.*

Agent: *I agree. That's one of the things the homeowner said, the school system is top-notch. Do you own this style of property?*

Neighbor: *Yeah, we've got a similar style. But we actually have an additional room on ours.*

Agent: *Oh, wow. That sounds lovely. Do you know how much your house is in today's market?*

Neighbor: *We have a general idea, but it's been a few years since an appraiser has been in.*

Agent: *Well, why don't I do this, if you don't mind? Why don't I find the time when I can come by, take a look at your house, and give you an idea how much your house is worth in today's market? You may be amazed.*

The whole point of this conversation—and the neighborhood open house itself—is to build rapport so that you can get in the door to see the neighbor's home.

I would also give the neighbors a packet when they leave, but this packet would be a little different than the one you would give a departing visitor at a public open house. Be sure to include information about the company and contact information, but also include a testimonial letter from the sellers of that listing stating why they decided to list with you and your company. You would request this letter from the sellers when they first hired you.

You could also include with the packet some kind of coupon that says "Free Over-the-Phone Market Analysis," meaning you could do this over the phone for them, giving them an idea of how much their house is worth. If they want a more specific pricing, you would need to come see the house. If you are somebody who's really tech savvy, or if somebody in your office is, use PowerPoint to make up a presentation about the company that you might use on listing appointments, take that CD, and put it in this packet.

So, anything that would be of value to a homeowner should be put in this packet and given to the neighbors as they leave. If you follow these steps, the neighborhood open house will be a successful event—one that should definitely generate some listing leads for you.

Old For Sale By Owners

The next prospecting vehicle to generate leads is old For Sale By Owners. These are people who tried selling their house several months ago, were unsuccessful in selling, and so stopped advertising. How would you go about finding out who they are? Current newspapers wouldn't have their ads. But if you were to go to the library, they would likely have all of the local newspapers for the last 12 months. So, go there and copy all of the For Sale By Owners for the last 12 months. Then put those ads in your file system and start making your calls. From this one source you could possibly generate hundreds of potential leads.

When you call, if the phone number has been changed or disconnected, don't try to find out the new number and, if you do find it, don't call it. No doubt the people have already moved—or, at the very least, they don't want to be contacted. Just move on to the next old For Sale By Owner. If that person is home and hasn't changed his or her number, it's likely that no move has taken place. So, maybe you can interest that person in what you have to offer. Here's the dialogue in calling all old For Sale By Owners:

Agent: *Hello, may I speak with Ms. Schaeffer?*

Owner: *This is she.*

Agent: *Well, hi. This is Darryl Davis from Power Realty. How are you?*

Owner: *Fine . . .*

Agent: *The reason I'm calling is because our records show that you tried selling your home many months ago. Is that correct?*

Owner: *Yes, we had it on the market for a while, but no one seemed very interested.*

Agent: *The reason I asked is because we had listed a lot of homes in your area around that same time you were trying to sell, and those homes did sell. Were you folks still planning to move any time soon?*

Owner: *We had hoped to.*

And then you just start asking questions:

Agent: *Let me ask you this, where were you folks thinking of moving to? . . . What time frame were you hoping too make the move by? . . . Why do you think the house didn't sell?*

You need to get clear about what their commitment is—why they were trying to move in the first place. In other words, ask them the same type of questions you would ask the For Sale By Owners. The real difference here is that you start with "I know you folks tried selling your house many months ago," whatever time frame it was, "and my company did list a lot of homes at that time that did wind up selling. I was just curious, why you think the house didn't sell?"

You could also say this:

Agent: *It's a shame that you folks didn't make that move. I'm assuming you were quite excited about it at the time. If I had a buyer who was willing to pay you the price that you wanted so you could make that move a success, would you consider selling your home again?*

You want to try and renew that interest.

This is the general conversation you should be having. As I've said elsewhere, the more calls you make, the more comfortable you will feel, and the more you will come up with your own questions and dialogue. But I strongly encourage you to try calling the old For Sale By Owners. They are a great vehicle for generating leads.

Absentee Owners

Some homeowners have a house but are not living there. May be they are renting the home to tenants. Or perhaps, for whatever reason, the home is vacant. To me, calling absentee owners is a great way to generate listing leads.

How do you find absentee owners? There are a number of ways to do so. One way is to check with your local Board of Realtors or Multiple Listing Services. See if they have the ability to search all the homes in your market for properties where the mailing addresses of the tax bills are different from the property addresses. Many Boards and MLSs will have this capability, depending on where you are conducting the search. Why do this search? Obviously, if the owners are getting their tax bills at mailing addresses other than the property addresses, they are not living at the properties.

Another and even easier way to find absentee owners is to go through the newspaper and look at ads for houses for rent. To me, this technique is awesome. Why? There are a lot of people who have watched programs on television about how to buy real estate with no money down, and some of them have gotten into investing in real estate. But a lot of these courses don't tell you how difficult it is to manage investment property. They don't talk about the negative side of owning investment real estate. Usually the positives out-weigh the negatives, especially in an "up" market, but many people who buy these no-money-down programs are part-time investors. It's often hard to be a part-time investor, because when there's some-thing wrong with the property that has to be fixed, or when the ten-ant moves out, the investor has to deal with those issues. The efforts to fix the problem or to fill a vacancy can be a real emotional drain for somebody, especially if he or she is a part-time investor.

The best time to call these part-time investors is when their houses require major repairs or when they are vacant, because the majority of these small investors do not have extra money to deal with the upkeep or vacancy of their properties. So, let's say a property owner is renting a house, and, if there is a positive cash flow, he or she does not take that positive cash flow and put the extra money into a sepa-rate bank account to use for a rainy day. When the repair problem or vacancy hits, this part-time investor then has to make both mortgage payments on his or her personal residence and either payments for repairs for the property that's in disrepair or another mortgage pay-ment on the property that's vacant. At this time the small investor is very motivated to get rid of the property and get out of this situation.

So look in the newspaper for "houses for rent" and call these home-owners. Here's the very simple dialogue you should use:

Agent: *Hi. I'm calling about the house for rent. My name is Darryl Davis from Power Realty. The reason I'm calling is that I notice you are trying to rent your property. But right now we're finding that it is a great time for investors who own real estate to actually wind up selling, because the market is changing and prices on properties are going up ... [or interest rates are changing or the market is changing or any one of a dozen reasons].*

That approach may be enough to persuade the owner to sell. But suppose the market is not good, and prices on properties are coming down. You could still do the dialogue like this:

Agent: *The reason I'm calling is that I noticed you are renting your house. We're finding that some investors are getting aggravated with having to deal with the rentals, and they have actually decided to sell their properties. So, I was wondering if you ever gave any thought to selling your property. I'm asking because I might have some people who would be interested in buying it.*

That would be the beginning of your conversation. Then you start getting into the same process of asking questions:

Agent: *How long have you owned the property? ... How much were you hoping to rent it for? ... If you were to sell it, how much would you want to sell it for?*

You can see how calling the absentee owners is a great way to generate listing leads.

Builders and Vacant Land

Another area where I've seen agents be very successful is working with builders and vacant land. But beware: if you focused exclusively on working with vacant land and builders (the two go hand in hand), you would be very unlikely to make a six-figure income your first year, because it takes some time and networking to break into this area.

Let's see how this works with an example. First, you have to do some serious investigative work to find the owner of a piece of vacant land. There's no house on the land, right? So, you've got to do the research to find out who owns the land and what the contact information is. Then you need to call them. If they are not interested in selling, perhaps you'd have to get them motivated to do so by telling them you have a builder who might be interested in that property for top dollar. So, working with builders and land is actually more like creating a listing and a sale at the same time that didn't exist before. Obviously, it's easier if there is a for-sale sign on the piece of land.

The other part of what you need to do is learn how to deal with variances, subdividing, getting utilities to the property, and the like. Builders want you to help them with that, and it's a whole other area of expertise.

The efforts involved in working with builders and vacant land are tricky, time consuming, and, often, expensive. But, depending on your market, this type of work can be very lucrative.

Let me share some thoughts on how you can break into this area of real estate. First, you need to make a list of all the local builders in your area. Don't start with the really large builders; they have their own team of agents they work with. Look for a small- to medium-sized builder. Once you've got that list, you need to start making a few calls to the builders and say, "Let me ask you a question. If I had a piece of vacant land, would you be interested in buying it?" Most probably you will find that builders will say, "Yeah, if you have something, let me know about it." So if you start finding land for some builders, they're going to love you for it and appreciate it. If you keep feeding one or two builders with land, all of a sudden they're going to look at you as their real estate agent. What might even start to happen is if they find land on their own and they need a real estate agent to help them get it sold, you would be the person they would call. I've seen plenty of agents make $100,000, $200,000, or even $300,000 a year in income just working land and builders. But again, it won't happen in the first year. You're going to have to go through a huge learning curve and struggle.

You should also start joining associations that focus on this aspect of real estate. Your Board of Realtors may have a chapter of developers exclusively or land exclusively, or both. You can join the Urban Land Institute (www.uli.org), the National Association of Home Builders (www.nahb.org), and Realtors Land Institute (www.rliland.com). You really need to get educated. I'm not saying you should focus on this area, but if you want to go this route, it is a great route, it's a competitive route, but it's going to take some time to negotiate the learning curve.

Community Groups

Keep in mind that the purpose of self-promotion is to have people know your name, face, and what you do for a living. So the more involved you are in your community, the better it is for you.

A great place to generate listing leads is your church, synagogue, or whatever house of worship you belong to. Join the groups there and also attend meetings of your local Chamber of Commerce, which is another place to get listings. If you have children, my favorite place to get involved is the school system. Participate in the local Parent Teacher Association (PTA); volunteer your time. This group needs the parents of schoolchildren to be actively involved, and if you're helping the school, you will get a lot of leads from the people you meet.

Here's an idea I'm fond of. A lot of schools use folders as a form of communication between parents and teachers. The teachers put homework assignments for the week in the folder, and then that folder goes home with the child to the parent. What usually happens with that folder is what happens in our home. That homework folder is sitting on our kitchen counter Monday through Friday. My son and I are going in there every day, pulling out the homework, doing it, reviewing it, and then it is sent back and forth between the teacher and my son (and, indirectly, to me). In this way, all three of us participate in the homework assignments, and the teacher and I can communicate our concerns about the work.

What I suggest you do is go to the principal and tell him or her you would like to sponsor the homework folders. You would offer to put the school logo on them, and your contact information would go on them, because you are sponsoring them. One company I recommend to make up these folders is www.schoolmate.com. Depending on the quantity ordered, the cost per folder could range from 80 cents to $1.50, which is not expensive when you consider the mileage you will receive from it. Think of how often people will see your company information when they use the folder on a daily basis. Other companies, too, could make up these folders; search in Google under "school folders."

Check out my Web site, www.NewAgentSuccess.com, for other prospecting ideas with community groups.

Farming

Another good way to generate listing leads is called "farming." Bear in mind: you, as a new agent, should *not* be focusing on farming. The best way for you to make a six-figure income your first year is by calling For Sale By Owners, expireds, old FSBOs, orphans, and doing the other things that I've covered up to this point. Nevertheless, farming does produce leads (a few years into your career, at least), so you should know how it works.

Farming, basically, consists of taking a group of people *whom you do not know* and marketing yourself to them on a regular, consistent basis. Unlike a "sphere of influence," which consists of people who know you, such as your friends and family, these are complete strangers you're going to be dealing with. You will be contacting them mostly by mail, although you can knock on their doors as well. People on your farm should be getting something from you at least once a month. By regularly contacting these people this way, after a period of time they will come to think of you when they think "real estate."

You've got to have people identify you much as they do brands in a store. For example, when people need to use a facial tissue, they usually think "Kleenex." They do so because Kleenex has such a hold on the market that their product is representative of their product category. Years ago, when somebody wanted to vacuum the carpet, he or she would say "can you get me the Hoover?" And a lot of people say, "May I have a Coke?" versus "Do you have a soda?" (or, in the Midwest, "pop").

So, when you have people think "real estate," you want them to think of you. And how do you do that? You've got to bombard them on a regular, consistent basis. And, after about a year to a year and a half of this effort, you will start getting great phone calls from people saying, "You know what? We've been getting your stuff," or "We've heard about you, we're thinking about selling. Could you come over and talk to us about listing our property?"

Keep in mind that farming is designed for future business. But most likely you need business *now*; otherwise, you won't have a future. I've seen brand-new agents go broke spending all of their money on farming. Don't fall into that trap.

Let's assume you are financially able to implement a farming campaign; here's how to do it. First, you need to create your list of people. In my opinion, you want to start with a minimum of 500 addresses. The concept is "more is better," because it's a numbers game. For example, let's say you had only five people in your farm and you mailed to these people once a month for a full year. What are the chances that you're going to make any money from just these five people? So, the more people you have in your farm, the better your chance is of getting a return on your investment. Let's say you start with 500 people you want to send mailings to on a consistent, regular basis each month.

How do you compile your list? There are several different approaches, but the best is by geography. You should look at where your office is and then you pick a neighborhood that's close to your office. You should definitely speak with your broker-manager about this matter, because there already may be some agents in the office who have a farm, and companies usually do not like more than one agent working a farm; it creates problems. When you speak with your broker-manager, she or he can help you to get the names and addresses for your farm.

What do you mail to the people on your farm? First, send a newsletter. There are some companies you can find in *REALTOR* magazine or through a Google search that will do newsletters for you. Second, you can also mail postcards, such as recipe cards, to people on your farm every month. The most popular item to mail each month are Just Listed and Just Sold information. Every time you list something, you would send out a notice that you just listed this property. You might be thinking, "Well, Darryl, I haven't listed anything yet." And that's why you shouldn't do farming until you have worked the For Sale By Owners and expireds, because that's the best way to start getting listings.

Mailing to people on the farm is going to cost you a good deal of money. If you have 500 people to whom you send mailings, it will cost you almost $200 each month just in postage. On top of that cost, you've got the cost of the making up the mailing. So farming is really for people who have been in the business for a while and already have a steady flow of income coming in from other avenues of listings.

But let's say you have the money to start farming but don't have any listings. What do you do then? You can send out a notice of a listing your office has just gotten or a sale the office has generated. You can also go to your Multiple Listing Service and use the listings and sales from there. The point is that every 30 days the same group of people is always seeing your name, looking at your face, and knowing what you do for a living.

After you have been mailing to people on your farm and bombarding them with mailings for a while, you could do some calls to them. Here's an example of one call you could make:

Agent: *Hi, this is Darryl Davis from Power Realty, how are you? I hope I've not interrupted you. The reason I'm calling is I've been sending you information about the market to keep you informed about what's going on in your neighborhood. Have you been getting it?*

Owner: *Yes, we have.*
(Whether they say "yes" or "no" doesn't matter. The point is to offer an additional service.)

Agent: *Well, one of things I'm also doing for my neighbors is I'm offering a free report called "How to Get the Most Value Out of Your Home." I understand you folks may not be selling right now, but if you ever do, this is a really great report that's good to have in your paperwork at home.*

Or you can say this:

Agent: *One of the things that we're offering as a service to the community is a free over-the-phone market analysis. Why we think this is real important is because for most people their home is one of the most important assets that they have. And just as you would do with a stock portfolio, periodically you should get an update on how your investment is doing. So, what we're offering is a simple, over-the-phone market analysis. How it works is I ask you some questions about the house, and then I go back to the computer, do a market analysis, and call you back with the results. Do you have some time for me to do this with you now? Are you interested?*

That's it! This approach is very simple, very basic. So, maybe twice a year with members of your farm, do a follow-up phone call, introduce yourself, and offer another kind of bonus service.

If you're inspired to knock on doors of people in your farm, I would wait for three to five months until people had been receiving mailings on a regular basis. Here are some reasons you can give for why you're stopping by:

- We just listed a new property, and I wanted to let you know about it.
- There's a new house for sale in their neighborhood, and I just wanted to let you know about it.
- Somebody just bought a home in the neighborhood, and I'd like to let you know about the new neighbors and what's going on.
- There's an open house in the neighborhood, and I'm stopping by to personally invite you to it.
- I work in the neighborhood and I was just wondering whether you are registered to vote, and, if not, may I help you with that?
- May I offer to do an updated market analysis for you?
- My company is sponsoring a charity, and I'm wondering whether you would like to contribute to that?
- There's a free report that may help to clarify some concerns you may have about the current real estate market. Would you like to look at it?

There are a lot of things you can offer or mention when you are knocking on doors. Once again, I would not do it until you've mailed them at least three to five times. That way, you already have a bit of name recognition when they see your face at the door. It's almost like you're a celebrity: "Oh, wow, I've been seeing you come in my mail every month."

Special Business Cards

The next item to help generate some listings leads is very simple idea. When you start listing property, you should have some business cards made up on your computer that you can print out from a color laser at the office or at an office services company like Kinko's. You're still going to order your regular business cards through your company, but you will also want to also print out your own on a very small run. Let's say you list a house for sale. What you do is take the photo of your new listing and a brief description of that property and print it on the back of your business card. So, on the front side you have your contact information, and on the back-side, a little billboard about your new listing. Do not put the price of the house on the card, because you want people to call to find out what the price is. You take these cards, and let's say you print out three dozen, you give them to the homeowner of the house that you just listed and say this:

> **Agent:** *I had these special business cards made up for you so that when you're out and about shopping or seeing friends and family, show them that you're selling your house; show them the picture and the little description of your house and tell them if they know of anybody who would be interested in more information they should give me a call.*

What's great about this promotion is that you actually have homeowners promoting you but they think they are promoting their houses. Even though this distribution of business cards seems like it is generating buyers, it will also generate sellers. For example, if somebody gets that business card and is thinking about selling, perhaps that person is going to call you now because of how creative you appear to be.

Advertising

A word about print advertising. I'm not going to get real deep into this, because as I mentioned in Chapter 2, advertising, particularly large advertising, is expensive, and you should not spend anything on advertising unless you have the money. I have seen plenty of agents go broke by spending way too much money on ads. Instead, invest your money in training courses or seminars that will improve your skill and ability. That's money well spent, because you need to learn this business. But as far as spending a lot of money on technology, advertising, mailings, and farming, don't do it unless you have the funds to do it.

One good thing about advertising is that you can create a perception that you've been in real estate for 50 years. To do that, go to your broker, or to another agent in your office, and tell him or her that you need to generate business. Ask the broker-manager if it's okay if you advertise his or her house for sale. In other words, you're going to pay for the ad, you're going to put your contact information in there, but it's the other agent's house (and commission); you might be able to generate some calls from buyers who have seen your ad. You don't really want the buyers, for reasons I have made clear elsewhere. The real purpose for making up the ad is that you can show it to homeowners when you go on your first few listing appointments. When they see your face, the ad, and 3, 4, or 10 homes for sale on this one-page ad, and you have two or three months of that kind of advertisement with you, naturally they are going to assume that those are your listings and that you have been in the business for years. So you do this primarily to position yourself and create the perception that you've been in real estate for a while.

Another great place to advertise is in a homeowners association paper. In your market there may be some gated communities. If there are, they most likely have a homeowners association paper they publish every month. Advertising in these papers is usually very inexpensive. What's great about this type of advertising is that if you "break into" a gated community, it starts to create a momentum of referrals.

If you belong to a church or a synagogue that has some kind of publication or newsletter, definitely advertise in that. Believe it or not, I know some people who, when they see that you've advertised in, say, a church bulletin, they automatically think you're a good person. It is a great advertising vehicle, and it's extremely inexpensive.

One of the biggest mistakes agents make when it comes to creating an ad or flyer is that they don't know how to use fonts properly. I've seen agents use several different fonts in an ad or they use just one. Here's the marketing rule of thumb when it comes to advertizing. You should never use fewer than or more than two fonts. You can take those two fonts and massage them: make them bold, italics, different sizes, but never use more than or less than two types of fonts. Also, one should be a blocky style, a sans serif font, meaning that it doesn't have ornamentation—little lines at the ends of letters; popular sans serif fonts include Helvetica and Arial. The other font should be something that has character, a serif font, meaning that it does have those little ornamental lines at ends of characters; commonly used serif fonts are Times New Roman and Century Schoolbook.

Also in your ads, make sure that you tell the reader to call you. For example, say "call today" or "call this number now." So, have a call to action, just like you see in television ads. They say, "Call now while supplies last. Call now, time is running out." Create a sense of urgency.

Most importantly, in any advertising you do, put your photo in it. If you don't have a good photo of yourself that represents you, go get one. You need to do that, as it's very important that people be able to identify you at a glance.

So, these are the techniques you can use to generate leads other than For Sale By Owners. The next chapter is going to go into other listing and selling techniques you can use on the listing appointment, but I highly recommend that you review these things, get good at them, and pick one or two items to attack. Which ones are going to be the most productive for you right now? I believe them to be the expireds, orphans, and old FSBOs. And it goes without saying that the FSBOs are most important, so review Chapter 7. Those are where your focus should be. There is a lot of business out there. Most agents do not pursue these sources. And if they do, they don't follow up. They're just not consistent. So use these techniques, be consistent, and work it. I promise you, you will be on track to make a six-figure income in your first year.

CHAPTER 9

The Listing Conversation

By now, you have gotten a lot of listing appointments. So, what do you do on the listing appointment? Let's go through the process of delivering the communication to a homeowner. My approach, what I teach my students, is how to list For Sale By Owners, because they are the hardest to list. If you have somebody who's a friend or a family member, or a referral, those are a lot easier. The For Sale By Owners are the toughest and so that's what I teach, because my theory is if you can list the toughest in our business, then the rest is a walk in the park.

Let me just say something about why I call it the "listing conversation." The term in our industry is "listing presentation," but I like to call it conversation, and here's why: people don't like to be sold. Sellers and buyers in today's market are way too sophisticated. As a matter of fact, the more they feel you're trying to sell them, the more defensive they become. So what you want to do on a listing appointment with sellers is you don't want to close them, you don't want to sell them. Instead, you want to have a conversation with them. There are a few things that you should be committed to in this conversation. What you need to be committed to is educating the homeowners, advising them, and also inviting them to take action that's consistent with what they're committed to. So, if they are committed to selling their house and moving to Florida to be with the grandkids, then the action that's consistent with that is they should hire somebody who's licensed by the state to help them accomplish their goal. That would be you, the licensed agent. Above all, make this a *conversation!*

Listing Conversation Process

First, I'll give you the overview, and then I'm going to break down the whole process. Because I want you to be yourself when talking with homeowners, I teach the listing appointment using the acronym REAL: *R*apport, *E*ngage, *A*dvise, *L*ist.

REAL =

Rapport

Engage

Advise

List

Let's look at each of these in turn.

Step 1: Build rapport with homeowners. You can work for the best company, you can have the best technique, you can have the best visuals when you're talking to homeowners, but if they don't like you, they are not going to list with you. So it's real important that you like them and they like you.

Step 2: Engage them in conversation. You want homeowners to be actively participating in your conversation. They should be listening to you and seated on the edge of their chairs as opposed to sitting with their arms crossed, being defensive.

What's the best way for you to get people engaged in a conversation? As mentioned in Chapter 7, the best way to do so is by asking questions. There's a rule of thumb in selling anything, and that is that you need to have two ears and one mouth. You should communicate in that proportion. Listen twice as much as you speak. People like to talk and share, so when you let them talk, they feel connected to you; they like you. The other reason why it's important that you ask questions is not only to engage them but also to find out what they are committed to. Homeowners who are selling their house are not just selling their house; they are also trying to accomplish something. It might be to move to Florida to be with their grandkids or to go to warmer climate. It could be that they are downsizing or upgrading. So, there's a bigger picture here. It's not just about selling their house. It's about getting to the next level in their lives; the better understanding you have of what that next level is, the better you can serve them. The best way for you to find out what sellers are committed to, what they are trying to accomplish, is by asking questions. Later on in this chapter I'll give you some examples of what to ask.

Step 3: Advise them. In this step you're going to coach the homeowners based on what they're committed to. If they are looking to sell their house to move to Florida to be with the grandkids, the best advice you can give them is that they need to hire a real estate agent, preferably you. At this point, you need to open up with them, to share with them, to *advise* them. Here's what you bring to the table for your sellers, for your clients. Now is the time to use your listing conversation book. (Later on, I'll explain what I mean by conversation book.)

Step 4: List. This is the time when you actually fill out the listing agreement, when all is said and done.

Now let's examine what types of conversations should be taking place during each of these steps.

Conversation for Building Rapport (Step 1)

The first thing you want to do after you approach the house and you ring the doorbell is to give the homeowners a friendly greeting:

Agent: *Mr. and Mrs. Hunna-Hunna, I just want to thank you for giving me the opportunity to meet you folks face to face.*

Then, you want to take them to the kitchen table. How you do that is by simply walking directly to the kitchen table and placing your stuff down upon it. You want to have the conversation there, because that's where friends and family meet; it's the focal point of the family.

Go to the kitchen table, place your stuff on it—but don't sit down. You're now going to ask them something:

Agent: *Would you take me through the property?*

This house tour is a great opportunity for you not only to get educated about the house, see what they have, and start building rapport with the owners, but also to do a lot of *oohs* and *ahs* about the home. (This enthusiasm on your part will come in handy later on, when you talk with them about what their house is worth.) Let them know that you appreciate their home as much as they do; that you understand all the pluses that their house has:

Agent: *Oh, this feature is lovely! . . . Look at that workmanship! . . . Did you decorate yourselves? . . . Did you have that custom built? . . . Wow, this place certainly is roomy!*

These are the types of things you should be saying. No doubt your remarks will start a conversation. Whether they do or not, be sure to keep asking questions. That will help to build rapport.

During this stage, don't worry about Steps 2, 3, and 4. Don't worry about what's to come. Right now, just have fun and enjoy these people's company. Also make sure that both partners take you through the house, because this will help you to build rapport with both of them. If Mr. or Mrs. Hunna-Hunna doesn't want to do this tour with you, just kindly urge this:

Agent: *Please join us, because you may have some other insights and things to add, and I may need to ask you some questions. So, if you don't mind, come on through with us.*

Conversation for Engaging (Step 2)

After you have gone through the entire house, go back to the kitchen table. You're now going to engage them by asking them some questions about what they are trying to accomplish.

The following questions are some very basic ones you should be asking. You don't have to ask all of these questions (although

I think you should). You might even ask more. Remember, this is a "conversation." Don't make it sound like you're a police sergeant conducting an interrogation. Make it a two-way street.

- So where are you folks moving to? Why there?
- Have you looked at any houses yet in the area where you're moving to?
- In what price range are you looking?
- How long have you lived in this current house?
- When do you want to make this move by?
- Have you ever sold a home before? When was that?
- Did you ever work with an agent before in either buying or selling a home? (This is an important question, because if they say "yes," you can make an interesting point: they worked with an agent to buy their home, but when they're trying to sell it, they want to do it on their own to save the commission. Be sure just to hint at this; anything more explicit could be construed as an accusation. For example:

Owner: *Yes, we bought our house in Florida through an agent.*

Agent: *Oh—interesting. You bought through an agent but now you're trying to do this on your own.)*

- If you were to hire an agent, what characteristics would you look for?
- What is the next step in your marketing plan?
  (This question will often stump them, because homeowners don't usually have a marketing plan. Their "marketing plan" consists of just putting an ad in the paper. Whereas with you, you'll share *your* detailed, legitimate marketing plan.)
- What is most important to you? Is it price or time?
  (Nine times out of 10, the answer will be "price." Then you'll get the opportunity to demonstrate that price might not always be the most important thing. For example:

Owner: *Well, of course, price is most important.*

Agent: *So, let me just get clear on something. If it took you six months to sell your house in order to get your price, would that be okay?*

Seller: *Oh, no! No. We can't wait six months. We want to get down to Florida in the next three months.*

Agent: *So, in other words, Mr. and Mrs. Hunna-Hunna, time is most important. I do understand you don't want to give the house away and there's a certain number that you need to get to make this move work, but it's got to happen within the three months. Is that right?)*

The last question to ask will help you segue from Step 2 to Step 3.

- Let me ask you Mr. and Mrs. Hunna-Hunna, if I could help you get to $250,000 with the monies that you need to make this move a success, would that be of interest to you?
  (That's a simple question—and a great one. They'll almost always say, "Well, yeah, if you can get us what we need and get us to $250,000, we'd be interested in working with you in some fashion. But we're not listing.")

Now you go on to Step 3.

Conversation for Advising (Step 3)

During the advising stage of the process, you will need to bring with you visual materials of some kind. Why? You'll find that people will become more engaged with you when you have visuals to show them. Also, you'll create a good impression if you have some kind of professional-looking materials on hand. It will add to your credibility if you can show as well as describe what you do. You'll also find that having visuals available will be particularly helpful during those appointments with people who are primarily visually (as opposed to verbally) oriented.

These are all valid reasons for having visual materials with you when you are at the advising stage. But what kind should you bring? Some agents I know actually make up a PowerPoint slide show and bring that with them on the appointments. That's fine . . . for them. I personally don't like to do this, for two reasons. Number one, as soon as you boot up a computer, it looks very formal. From there on in, it's not a conversation, it's a presentation. Number two, it's very cumbersome to use PowerPoint. I sometimes find it difficult, even in my own seminars, to jump from, say, slide 5 to slide 15. Why introduce awkwardness in the listing conversation?

What I like to use is the listing conversation book. With a book, after a while, you start to know what visuals are on what pages, so you can jump around and refer to pages very easily. The homeowners wouldn't even see you jumping from, say, page 5 to page 15; the transition would be seamless. So, let's see how to put together a listing conversation book.

The Listing Conversation Book

For the best organization, your listing conversation should be set up into four sections. The first section would be your credentials and your background—everything and anything about you. If you're a new agent, you might be thinking to yourself, *I don't have a lot of credentials*, but you really do.

You can put many items in this section of your listing conversation book that shows your credentials. For example, you ought to put in a copy of your real estate license. Likewise, include a duplicate of the certificate you received when you joined your local Board of Realtors, and if you belong to the local Board, you automatically belong to the State and the National Association of Realtors. By the way, I highly recommend that you get active in your local Board of Realtors and join a couple of committees, especially committees that would be relevant to buyers and sellers. For example, when I was an agent, I was the chairman of the Professional Standards Committee, and I explained to a homeowner on a listing appointment that if a homeowner ever had a complaint about an agent, it would be sent to my committee. So technically my responsibility was policing our Code of Ethics. That was a very powerful credential, because a homeowner would perceive me as being very ethical—perhaps the most trusted agent that they could work with.

The following are some other items that you could include in this section:

- Certificates you received from other training programs you have taken
- Community activities in which you are involved
- A copy of your Code of Ethics

You want to explain to homeowners that being a member of the National Association of Realtors means that you subscribe to a Code of Ethics and that there are a couple of articles in the code that speak directly to the fiduciary responsibility you have to sellers to be honest.

The second section of your listing conversation book should be information about your company. Some companies teach their agents that company information should be in the first section of the book, but I like to have it in the second for the simple reason that homeowners have to buy into *you* first. If the homeowners don't buy into you, they are not going to buy into anything that you say about your company either. So you first have to establish credibility about yourself, and then you add credibility about your company.

If you belong to a franchise, you would include information about the franchise in this second section, and be sure to point out this information to homeowners and talk about it during the listing conversation. Some franchises promote how many houses they have sold, how long the company has been around, or even how many agents they have—in other words, the bigness of the franchise. You could do that as well in the book; it never hurts to be identified with a big, trustworthy, credible organization. At this point in the book, just concentrate on the credibility and bigness of the franchise. Leave any information about how the franchise gives exposure to a property for sale and the national advertising that the franchise does until Section 3, which deals with marketing.

Whether or not you are a member of a franchise, be sure to include in this second section information about the individual company you work for. Some of the items might be the mission statement (if the company has one), a picture of the staff, and a picture of the broker-manager. Take a lot of pictures of the office and put them in the book. Give homeowners a virtual tour of the office. Keep in mind that real photos always work better than stock photos. For example, a photo of you standing in front of a for-sale sign on a piece of property you sold would be more effective than a franchise company stock photo of a for-sale sign in a front yard (and that photo, of course, would go in Section 3 of the book).

The third section of your listing conversation book is your marketing plan. This part is where you talk about all of the tools and techniques that you use to get property sold. This is the time when you need to talk about what you do to market properties. In Section 3 of the book, you'll include sample feature sheets, any forms or tools you use to stay in communication with homeowners, broker opinion sheets, public open house checklists, open house for the public guest sign-in sheets, mortgage information, advertising that you do, and brokers' open house pictures. In other words, include visuals of all the things you do to get a property sold for homeowners.

The fourth section is a miscellaneous section where you can just throw in things that you probably wouldn't use in the other three sections unless a question comes up. It's just back-up stuff, things that you may not talk about on a regular basis on every appointment.

Overview of the Advising Stage of the Appointment

Once you have your listing conversation book prepared and have reviewed materials and information, you're ready to begin the listing conversation in earnest—you're ready to give advice. Bear in mind, all listing conversations are different. People's needs, wants, reactions, and emotions are all different, and they affect the dynamics of the conversation. So, it's impossible to say *exactly* what will go on in a listing conversation or how long it will last. (My appointments have lasted anywhere from 60 minutes to two hours or more.) What follows is an overview of what generally goes on during a conversation. You'll learn more about what to say and will fine-tune your technique after you have had some experience with actual conversations. I strongly recommend attending a training program for fine-tuning your techniques.

Recall that during the listing conversation you have asked the homeowners, during the previous step (Step 2: engaging), whether you can help them get to Florida with the monies they need to make the move a success. Here's how to handle a positive reaction:

> **Seller:** *Yes, we would definitely be interested if you could help us with that.*
>
> **Agent** (*turning to the first page Section 1 of the listing conversation book*): *Great! But first, Mr. and Mrs. Hunna-Hunna, let me share some information about me. I think that it is important that you understand who I am, what I do, and how I got into this business. So, let me give you a little background . . .*

Now is the time to share with the homeowners your credentials. This part of the conversation should take less than five minutes. After your personal credentials are established, turn to Section 2 of the listing conversation book and share the credentials of your company. Again, this part of the conversation should take less than five minutes.

Then turn to Section 3 of the listing conversation book, which illustrates for homeowners what you do to market properties. Discuss with them what you intend to do to market *their* property. Plan to spend at least 20 minutes on this part of the conversation.

This is where most agents are weak on a listing appointment. Most agents merely educate homeowners; they don't really deliver the message in a powerful way that causes the homeowners to say, "Yes, I need this. Yes, that's different. I can't do that. This will put more money in my pocket than if I did it on my own. Yes, this will bring more buyers through my property than doing it on my own." Homeowners need to be thinking such a thing if you hope to get the listing from them.

To actually get the listing, you need to validate the power of what you do as a real estate agent. And you need to do that by comparing yourself to the real estate industry as a whole. We all have the same tools at our disposal: brokers' open houses, advertising, yard signs, and so on. Every agent uses his or her tools in different ways. Some are better at it than others. You need to explain how you're different from the pack and how you will get the sellers to a sale. For example, let's say the homeowners raise the objection about not having success with an agent in the past; here's how you should respond:

Seller: *We've tried working with agents before, it didn't work. We tried multiple listing.*

Agent: *If I were to take two licensed builders, they both basically have the same tools at their disposal. They have hammers, screwdrivers, and nails. If you gave these two different builders the same tools, you're going to get two different results. Why? Because they will use the tools in different ways. Some will do it better than others. But if one house comes out shoddy and the other one comes out great, you don't blame the hammer, the screwdriver, or the nails. So, all real estate agents that belong to our Board of Realtors basically have the same resources to get a property sold, but how they use those resources is where the uniqueness comes in.*

At this point, you need to validate yourself by following through on a process I call "FEA." FEA stands for *Feature, Explain,* and *Advantage,* and it's a great way to achieve success at this stage. I use it in my training courses and have found that the better the agent is at FEA, the higher the commission. Here's how you explain each one of the marketing tools that you can use for homeowners.

First up is *Feature*: simply make a statement about what you will do to market the property. Then you need to *Explain* what the marketing entails. Finally, you need to express the *Advantage* of using your time-proven techniques to get the property sold as quickly as you can and at the price that the sellers are asking for it. Many agents have proven to be weak at this Advantage point. You need to make it absolutely clear what the advantage is to homeowners of using a particular marketing tool, in terms of time and money saved. And you need to point out the disadvantages to them if they don't avail themselves of the marketing tool you are describing.

FEA =

Feature

Explain

Advantage

Let's see how this works, using an example. Say that the marketing tool that you want to highlight and explain is the Multiple Listing Service.

(Note: I just refer to the Multiple Listing Service in my seminars as "the List"; you can do so as well, but be sure to use the full name of the service the first time you mention it to the homeowners.)

Before you go on the listing appointment, print out from your Multiple Listing Service the online version of all the homes that are currently for sale in your market. Say that you opt to sort it first by town, then by ascending price. Here, then, is how you would present the Multiple Listing Service using FEA:

Agent: *Mr. and Mrs. Hunna-Hunna, one of the reasons why homeowners selling on their own won't sell for as much as we can as real estate agents is because of the Multiple Listing Service. Are you familiar with it? (This takes care of the Feature part.)*

Seller: *No. (It doesn't matter whether the answer is "no" or "yes," continue anyway.)*

Agent: *You see, when you hire an agent, they'll put your home on the Multiple Listing Service. Immediately all of the members of our Board will now know that your house is for sale. So if we have a thousand members, that's a thousand agents already aware of your property; it's a very powerful tool.*
(That takes care of the Explain part.)

Seller: *Sounds impressive.*

Now to move on to the all-important Advantage.

Agent: *Now, the type of buyer that you want to attract is obviously somebody who can afford your house, correct? The person or people you have in mind are no doubt going to be based on the type of home you are selling. Most likely the people you are picturing are a married couple, with perhaps one or two children. This married couple will both be working, probably Monday through Friday, nine to five. That type of financially secure, serious buyer will not have the time to look in the paper, circle ads, and call homeowners directly to make their own appointments. That process is very cumbersome.*

Seller: *I hadn't thought of that.*

Agent: *The same thing applies to the employer who wants to hire somebody. There are two ways to do it. The employer can either place the ad him- or herself and do all the interviews, or that person can just hire an employment agency to do the research and send the best of the best. You get what you pay for.*

Okay, so the type of buyers that you want, they're not going to have the time to scour through ads, circle the ones that interest them, and make appointments to check out the properties. It's easier for them to go to an agent and say, "I want this type of property. . . . I'm looking for these features. . . . I'm interested in these things. When you find all these things, call me."

At this point, that agent they hired to find them their house goes to the list of available homes. Now, Mr. and Mrs. Hunna-Hunna, let me show you this List. Each line represents one house for sale, so there are about 30 homes on each page. . . .

At this point you go through the Multiple Listing Service printout and flip through the pages, saying things like, "Look at this," "This is great," "Check this out," and so on. Pique their interest:

Agent: *... Now here's what happens. The buyer says, "I want this, this, and this," and the agent goes to the List to look for that house. Now when they go to the List, Mr. and Mrs. Hunna-Hunna, do you know what they don't see?*

Seller: *What?*

Agent: *They don't see your house. In my opinion, by you not being on the List, it's like you're not even on the market. Bear in mind, I'm not saying this because I want you to list with me. As a matter of fact, if you don't feel good about me, I don't want you to hire me. What I am trying to communicate is that this is one of the most powerful tools that an agent brings to the table for you, and if you don't feel good about me, then I encourage you to find another agent, because you need to get on the List.*

You see that the type of buyers who go to an agent are the type of buyers who are committed to buying a house. They know that the agents have the majority of the homes for sale. The type of buyers who will go through the headaches and troubles of cutting out ads and making their own appointments are the ones who are more committed to saving money. The buyers who work with an agent know they may be paying top dollar, because they know there's a commission built into the price, but they don't care about that. They care about finding the right home. They're more committed to finding a house that works for them than trying to save money.

So, the people advertising on their own, the type of buyers they are attracting are more of the thrifty kind, who are looking to save a nickel. What happens with these folks is that, no matter what you are asking, they are always trying to want to talk you down in price.

Seller: *We've had a lot of those lately.*

Agent: *No doubt you have. So, do you see the advantage of the Multiple Listing Service and getting on the List? Once you get on the List, the agent's job is to make sure that your house jumps out from all the other homes that are currently for sale. Now, here's how I do it. The next thing we do is the broker's open house....*

Continually validate the power of each particular marketing tool that you mention. You need the homeowners to get to the point where they say, "Yes, I need that. I really do." If you do that, by the time you're done, the last part of the conversation with them about their listing with you will be so much easier.

At this point, it's time to talk about presenting price. To do so, you'll need to have on hand your market analysis and printouts of listings of similar homes in the area that have sold. Let's review how this market analysis is put together before we get into the actual listing conversation about price.

Before you go over to the house, you need to look at what similar properties have sold for. There are a couple of ways to do that, and each office has a little different approach. Most likely you'll be going through the Multiple Listing Service and looking at a one-month to a six-month time frame of all the properties in the same school district that have sold and are similar to this property. I won't go into specifics here of how the analysis is done; the details may vary a bit depending on the individual situation. But the traditional approach is to pull up three properties that have sold, three properties that are currently for sale, and three properties that were for sale but never sold. Then, through comparison and averaging, the agent comes up with a fair price for that type of house in a particular market area.

My advice to you is to not do it that way. Why? First, you are including the three houses that didn't sell, but *why* didn't they sell? Most likely they didn't because they were overpriced. If you were to show the homeowners the listings for these overpriced properties, all that would register with them would be the high numbers. You can tell them that the houses are overpriced, but it doesn't matter. When they look at those numbers, they will start thinking, *My house is worth more than I originally thought!*

Second, you might find the same situation with properties that are currently for sale. Some properties might have been for sale for a long time, perhaps for the same reasons that the never-sold homes were.

It would be better for you to include just the sold properties in your market analysis and listing printout, and you don't have to limit yourself to just three. In fact, the more houses that you include, the better. I wouldn't show homeowners 20 or 30 listings for similar houses that have sold; that would be overkill. Instead, limit yourself to showing listings for five to seven homes. Keep pointing out how much the homes have sold for and when:

Agent: *Here's a house similar to yours that sold for $315,000 in two months. . . . Here's another one that sold for $310,000 in just three weeks. . . . This beauty sold for $320,000 in about a month. . . . This one for just under $315,000 was on the market for just a short time, about a week, I think. . . . And this house for $305,000 was snapped up in a few days.*

If you present the homeowners with all these properties that have sold for between $300,000 and $320,000, but they are asking for $350,000, obviously they would see that they are pricing their property for more than most buyers are willing to pay. Before you actually present the price, and even before you go on appointments, ask your broker or manager if he or she can ask some bank appraisers if they can make a request, in writing, for comparables of two or three properties they are currently working on appraising. You'll want to do that so you can take a copy of these letters with you on the listing appointment to show the homeowners.

With these things done and with the necessary documents on hand, you're ready to begin to present pricing in the listing conversation:

Agent: *Mr. and Mrs. Hunna-Hunna, I just spent the past hour or so talking about what we need to do to market your house for sale. At this point, it's important that we choose the correct price to put it on the market at. Let me explain why. Let's say that we ask more for the house than what it's worth. In this example, let's say we ask $500,000 and some silly buyer comes along and pays that high price. What now happens is the buyer goes to the bank and asks for money. The bank sends out an appraiser to make sure that the property is a good investment. The bank appraiser says, "Oh, my gosh, it's not worth $500,000." The bank appraiser tells the bank, the bank tells the buyers, and all of a sudden the deal falls apart.*

The real drawback of this whole process is that it may take a month to a month and a half to happen. So, what we've done is we've taken the property off the market for about a month and a half, losing valuable marketing time. Even if we could sell it to an uneducated

*buyer for more than what it's worth, we don't want to do that, because
we'll never see that money. Do you follow me?*

Seller: *So far ...*

Agent: *So what I've done is I've pulled the comparables that the
bank appraiser is actually going to look at. By the way, let me show
you something first. Here are a couple of letters from bank appraisers
calling my office, asking for comparables. The reason why bank
appraisers are calling my office is because my office is so active in the
marketplace, we're the ones making the comparable home prices, the
comps. You see, real estate agents do most of the sales that happen in
our community. So what we're going to look at right now is the same
data that the bank appraiser is going to look at. So we've got a jump
on this and now we're going to make an educated decision.*

By saying this to the homeowners, you have validated your comps
before you have actually shown them. Now what I suggest you do is
lay the comps out for the homeowners to look at and discuss them:

Agent: *Here we've got a house for 300, here's another one at 310,
here's another one at 305, here's one at 315, here's one at 302. So it
looks like we're in this 300 to 315 range. Based on what you see
here, Mr. and Mrs. Hunna-Hunna, what do you think would be a
good price on your property?*

Seller: *We were thinking we could get $330,000.*

Agent: *Keep in mind that the higher we go, there will be fewer
buyers interested in it. Therefore, it might take a little longer at that
price. But if you're willing to try it, I'm willing to try too, as long as
we understand that it may take a little bit longer.*

So that's how you would present the price of the home.

Conversation for Getting the Listing (Step 4)

Once you have an agreement on the asking price, you're going
to start filling out the listing agreement. Assume a lot; don't
ask the homeowners, "Are you ready to hire me? Do you want to
sign the form?" You don't want to do that, because they'll say "no."
So after you've talked about the price, then you just take the

form out, you've got your pen in your hand, and ask them something else:

Agent: *Let me just get some information. What's today's date?*

Seller: *It's the fifteenth of the month. I ... (seeing the agent starting to fill in the form) What are you doing? I don't know if we are ready to move forward on it at this time.*

At that point, you will handle any objections or concerns they have, but for the most part, just assume that there won't be any objections. After all, you have just spent the past hour or two with these homeowners building rapport, understanding what they are committed to, coaching them, and suggesting to them what they need to do to get the property sold.

As you're filling out the form, you don't want there to be a lull in the conversation. If there is silence, the homeowners will start to think, *Oh, my gosh. Are we doing the right thing? Are we rushing it?* So try to keep the homeowners involved. Some agents have given them other paperwork to fill out or to read. Others, as they are filling out the form, still talk to the homeowners by saying things like, "So are you going to be using this furniture? Are you planning on getting new furniture in this move?"

When you're finished filling out the form, hand the form and the pen to one of the sellers. I think that it's best to first give it to the seller with whom you feel you have the most rapport. That will give you a better chance of having the document signed quickly without any objections or further discussion. And when one homeowner signs, it's easier for the second one to do so also. While you're getting one of them to sign, you need to distract the other one. Whatever you do, don't give one partner the opportunity to ask permission of the other to sign; don't let the "honey, what do you think we should do?" question be reached.

Let's say you have better rapport with Mrs. Hunna-Hunna. Here's how the conversation should go from here:

Agent: *Mrs. Hunna-Hunna, just okay the form there. So Mr. Hunna-Hunna, let me ask you, do you actually use the workbench downstairs, or did you inherit that from the previous owner? I'm asking because I'm not handy at all, and I admire people who are.*

Mr. Hunna-Hunna: *Oh, I do my own woodworking. I find that it relaxes me, and it keeps my mind sharp. I manage to get down* *there a couple of times a week for a few hours, which I really enjoy . . . .*

While you and Mr. Hunna-Hunna are talking, Mrs. Hunna-Hunna is signing. When she's done, move the form to Mr. Hunna-Hunna, and ask him to sign. The same thing happens in this situation: while the one partner is signing, ask the other whatever questions would be appropriate based on the conversation that you have had:

Agent: *(as Mr. Hunna-Hunna is signing the form): So, Mrs. Hunna-Hunna, are you excited about making this move and the house you found?*

Mrs. Hunna-Hunna: *Well, you know, we are concerned about the logistics of it all. But, yes, we are very excited about getting into a bigger place. And we both just love the area we're moving to . . .*

Keep the conversation going like this until both homeowners have signed the form. This is somewhat manipulative but not too much so, because the truth of the matter is that if they don't like you, they're not going to list with you. You cannot make people do anything they don't want to. But what you do want to do is manage any stuff "in their head" where they start to have second thoughts. When people get to the point of feeling like they are being closed on something, even like buying a car, fear kicks in. They may want a car, need a car, and like that car that they are going to buy, but when push comes to shove, when it comes to signing a legal document, they start to get extremely uncomfortable. Even though it's the best decision or the right decision for them, fear consumes them, and then no action is taken. So all you're doing is making sure that any fears or concerns the homeowners have don't consume them and keep them from taking action. They need to move forward on the decision of what they should do, which in this case is to get their house on the Multiple Listing Service with you and your company so that you can market and sell it.

Handling Objections

Throughout the listing appointment, you will be getting objections from homeowners from time to time. These are some of the common ones I've heard:

- We don't want to commit right now; we want to sleep on it for a couple weeks.

- We're not sure we want to go with you; you see, we have a friend in the business . . .
- Why should we go with you? The other agent said she will do it for less commission.

A whole seminar could be devoted to this one topic (and, as a matter of fact, I have done just that). In the interests of keeping this simple, I have given you the foundation on how to do a listing conversation and covered some of the basic objections and how to handle them. As you go on several appointments and start to get several objections, you'll learn more about how to handle them. I suggest that, once you have had a little experience with the listing appointments, you go through a training program about how to handle the objections. Make sure to check out www.NewAgentSuccess.com; it includes tips on handling objections that will help you on the listing appointments.

Playing with Buyers

Up to this point, I've covered the listing conversation with For Sale By Owners and expireds. As I've said repeatedly, these are the people you should be focusing on; they are the ones who bring in the real money. But, realistically, until you've gotten at least six listings and you're on track to make a six-figure income, I know you're going to still wind up taking some buyers out.

If you do that, keep in mind the warning that I mentioned at the beginning of the book. Most new agents get in the trap of starting out with listings but switching to buyers when they find out how much work is involved with listings. Soon that "taking a break" mentality becomes life work and they never go back to the lucrative listings again. Don't get lured into this trap. Make your work with buyers temporary or incidental—not a habit, and certainly not a career.

So, without further ado, I'm going to give you some dos and don'ts in playing with buyers. That's what I call it: *playing*, not *working*. To me, work is getting on the phone, calling For Sale By Owners and expireds, and getting listing appointments. With buyers, you take them out, put them in your car, show some property, and either they buy a house or they don't. To me that's not work, that's play, and you get paid proportionately for it.

Categorizing Buyers

The first thing to do with buyers is put them into categories: A, B, or C. An A buyer is somebody who *has* to buy; a B buyer is somebody who *wants* to buy; and a C buyer is somebody who *would like* to buy. A C buyer is basically a window shopper. Stay away from this type of buyer. B buyers may be committed to buying, but there's no sense of urgency with them. When they find the right house, they'll move forward on it. The A buyer is the one who is committed to buying—and in a relatively short period of time. This type of buyer has to buy, and there are no ifs, ands, or buts about it.

Obviously, the A category of buyer is the one I think you should focus on. That said, let's examine a typical profile of an A buyer. An A buyer is somebody who is going to be homeless in the next 60 or 90 days. This person may have just sold a house or may have a lot of cash and is renting. Or perhaps the A buyer's lease is about expire and she needs to move, pronto. It's a no-brainer; this person is going to buy something.

I suggest that with A buyers, you take them out and show them many properties; if they don't buy something, show them some more. In other words, you work the A buyer until she or he buys something.

To determine whether or not a buyer is in the A category, show the buyer a house the first time you meet him. If you see that he is interested but not really sincere about buying or is moderately interested but not in any rush, categorize him as C or B, respectively, and move on. Put the C and B category buyers in your file system to work them at a later date. The object is to stick with A buyers.

Showing Properties to Buyers

How to determine what properties to show a buyer? One of the things that I teach in all my seminars and my training courses is the shiny penny list. Here's how it works (and it does work—it will dramatically save you time with buyers). Let's say a buyer is looking to buy a house for $300,000, and let's say that in that price category there are many different homes. Suppose that there are 40 of them. Of those 40, perhaps a handful—five to seven of them—are going to be better than the rest. They will be better because they have more square footage for the price, they look better than the other homes, the location is more convenient, the school system is better—there could be any number of reasons. In other words it's got better value than the rest; it's got more bang for the buck. That's the shiny penny.

Look at it this way: if buyers can afford to buy a $300,000 house, are they going to buy the best house in their price range or the worst? Obviously, they are going to buy the best, even if the home is not in the style they think they wanted. If they say, "We want a colonial for $300,000" and there is a ranch that has more bang for the buck, I guarantee you, they're going to buy that ranch, because buyers want to buy whatever house is the best in their price range.

You should be keeping separate lists of properties: one for the listings in house and others for other brokers. Once you hear what price the buyer is looking for, you should go through your in-house inventory and other brokers' listings, select the ones that fit the price criteria you are looking for, and then clump them into separate price categories. For example, 300 to 325 would be one category (for houses listing for $300,000 to $325,000, respectively), 325 to 350 would be another (for houses listing for $325,000 to $350,000, respectively), and so on. So, you look at these categories and then pick the five to seven shiny pennies in those categories.

As a new agent, it's going to take you some time to learn value, to learn what shiny pennies are. But here's the concept. In your Multiple Listing Service there could be a thousand homes, but of the thousand, there are only a hundred shiny pennies. You create a separate list for yourself, and when you meet buyers for the first time and tell you the price range they are looking for, ignore what they tell you about the type of home they want. Why? Because they often say they want one thing and then end up buying something totally different. After all, if the buyers *really* knew what they wanted, they would have already bought it. They *think* they know, but what *we* know is that they want to buy the most house for their money— that's the shiny penny. So you take buyer out, and you show them just the one to seven shiny pennies in their category. You can do that in one day. If they don't buy one of those shiny pennies, what does that tell you about the buyers? It tells you they are probably not ready to buy.

So, if they don't buy one of the shiny pennies, you put them in your file system. The next shiny penny that comes up in their category, you call them and tell them to come out and see the new house. Very simple. Doing things this way will free up your time. You'll avoid doing what all the other new agents do when they have buyers who say, "I want to buy a house for $300,000"; they wind up showing every single house in the $300,000 price range. Servicing that one call can become a full-time career. The only exception to what I'm saying are the A buyers. You show the A buyers the shiny pennies and the non-shiny pennies, because you know they are going to buy something. With A buyers, you show everything.

Generating Appointments with Buyers

The last thing I want to address in playing with buyers is how you generate buyer appointments. Doing so is very simple. The more listings you have, the more buyer calls you're going to get. If you do what I've covered in this book, you're going to start to get a lot of listings; you're going to get a lot of buyer calls. I suggest that when you grow your business to this point, you take all of the buyers who are not A buyers and give them to another agent who hasn't read any of my material. Let that agent mess around with the B and C buyers. You stay focused on A buyers and listings.

One of the most common approaches to getting buyer leads, other than from your own listings, is called "floor time," although some offices call it "up time" or "duty time." Basically, it is sitting by the phones waiting for buyers to call in. That is the worst possible use of any agent's time, so avoid floor time (or whatever it is called) at all costs.

Another place to generate buyer leads is from yard signs. When you get a listing and you place a yard sign on the property, it's going to generate buyer calls. When you advertise your listings for sale, that's going to generate buyer calls. Open houses and public open houses are going to generate buyer calls. Finally, you'll just start getting buyer leads from people finding out that you're in real estate. You will be amazed once you start telling people that you're in real estate how many buyers are out there. But again, you don't want those. Don't get excited about those. You want sellers, that's where the real money is.

I'm going to give you some questions to ask all the buyers you meet, because you may be able to generate a listing appointment from buyers. Here's how the conversation should go:

Buyer: *I'm thinking about buying a house.*

Agent: *What price range are you looking in? ... Have you seen any houses you liked? ... Why you didn't buy one of those? ... Do you folks own or do you rent now?*

Buyer: *We own our place.*

Agent: *Do you currently have your house on the market?*

Buyer: *Yes.*

(If they say "no," that's obviously a potential appointment for you. If they say "yes," then you want to clarify that.)

Agent: *Do you have it listed with an agent or are you trying to do it privately?*

Buyer: *We're trying to do it privately.*

Agent: *Is it still on the market?*

Buyer: *Yes.*

Agent: *May I make a suggestion to help you folks in coordinating the buying and selling of your home? What I'd like to do is find the time when I can come over and take a look at your house. By doing that we can accomplish basically three things. Number one, I can tell you exactly what your neighbors' homes have been selling for recently, and that's always a great gauge as to how much your house is worth. Number two, you may have a price that you're asking now and you want that number regardless of what you're neighbors have been selling for. Based on the number that you want, we can determine the timing of how long it'll take for you to sell your home and coordinate it with the purchase of the new one. Number three, which will be the main thing we'll accomplish, is that I want you to take me through your house and show me everything you like about it and everything you don't like about it, and that will give me a real clear picture of the type of house you're looking for.*

So for all the buyers you meet, if they have a property to sell and that property is in your general market area, you can turn it into a listing appointment.

For further information on how to work with buyers, I suggest that you check out my book *How to Become a Power Agent in Real Estate* or attend one of my live training programs.

So that is the general overview on how to work with buyers; but once again, focus on listings, not showing property. Don't work with buyers until you have gotten at least your first six listings.

CHAPTER 10

Your First 90 Days of Success

To wrap up, let me share with you some ideas of what you should be doing in your first 90 days of your real estate career. Be sure you go to my Web site, www.NewAgentSuccess.com. I am always creating new material for new agents, so you might find some business plans on that site that will help you.

Number 1: Your Mailing List

The first and most important thing is to sit down and create a mailing list of all the people you know: your friends, your family, your colleagues, people you went to school with, people you worked with in your previous career, everybody and anybody. Put that contact information into a file system of some kind, preferably some kind of contact management software. It will make you more efficient, more effective, and more organized. If money is tight, then try and make do with what you have. You do not, as I've said before, need a lot of technology to make a six-figure income. It does help to have it, it makes things easier, but you don't need it to succeed.

Number 2: Your Mailing

The next thing is to send a simple letter telling everyone on your list of your new career. Let them know that you are excited about it and you are there to help them if they need help with real estate matters; ask if they know of anybody who is thinking about buying or selling real estate and request that they contact you.

Number 3: Follow Up

The next thing is to create some kind of follow-up letter or mailing piece. Include anything about the real estate industry that might be of interest to somebody who owns a house: interest rates are going up, interest rates are going down. there's some new government notice, there are new tax concerns, and so on.

Number 4: Multiple Listing Service Research

Go look at other agents' properties that are on the Multiple Listing Service. Get a notebook and take notes as you go through the properties; doing so will help you remember these properties. I suggest maybe doing five houses a day, five days a week, for two weeks. That will give you about 50 homes under your belt. Make sure that you get a map of your local area so that you can learn the ins and outs of all the streets.

Number 5: Educate Yourself!

Take advantage of all the terrific and varied real estate training seminars that come to your area. Check with your local Board of Realtors and your Multiple Listing Service and find out about all the classes and seminars they have. Stay involved in being educated, even outside of your Board of Realtors. Any time a speaker comes to your area, make sure you go. Every time you do, you are going to learn something, and you are going to network with other agents; it's one of the best uses of your time.

Create some kind of system to keep track of all the things you learn from the seminars you attend. For example, agents that attend my training programs receive a manual that includes everything that I know about real estate. It's an incredible program, and the manual they receive has tabs that break up the real estate industry based on skill and things that are needed to be taught and learned. For example, it includes tabs about prospecting and the listing appointment, but there's also self-promotion, technology, handling objections, servicing listings, and so on.

Create a binder for yourself with categories of the industry, and whenever you go to any seminar, make sure you take those notes and file them behind the appropriate tab. That way you can always go back and refer to it.

Number 6: Take Advantage of Company Tools

Become familiar with all the tools your company has. Get some professional photos. Make sure that you order your business cards and stationery with your photo on them. Put together your listing conversation book. In Chapter 9, I told you how to do it. I also recommend that you ask other agents in your office to see what they do on a listing appointment. Find out what they bring with them. Also, make sure you put your file system in place for calling For Sale By Owners and expireds. Either use the contact management software or use the hard file system that I discussed in Chapter 5.

Number 7: Stay Motivated!

Congratulations for reading this book. I know that it took a lot of time and energy. This material did not cover every possible scenario. There's no book that can cover every situation, especially for a new agent. But here's what I can promise you. If you stay diligent and stay committed to being educated, this is the best profession you can be in. I have seen so many people who have achieved the next level in their lives because of this career. It's helped many people get out of bad situations. This career, this industry, this profession is a tool for you to get to your next level. And if you are good to it, it will be good to you. It can give you endless riches, which might sound a little hokey, but it's true. It will only give you as much as you are committed to achieving.

Number 8: Don't Let Fear Get in Your Way

I welcome you to our profession. I truly wish the best for you. Please push past any fears that you have. If I were sitting across from you and you were a brand-new agent and you were asking me, "Darryl, what's the one thing that I've got to be aware of, or what's the one last bit of advice you would give me?," it would be this: it's okay to have fear, but don't let fear have you. If there's one thing that has killed countless dreams and killed off possibilities for people it is fear. As you go through this business, you will have fear. You'll have the fear of rejection, the fear of not knowing what to say, the fear of the unknown, and that's all normal. Just don't let it paralyze you or hold you back.

Closing Thoughts

The last thing I'm going to leave you with is a piece I use to close out all my seminars. I hope this inspires you as much as it does me—I actually decided to become a speaker after reading these words from George Bernard Shaw.

A Splendid Torch

This is the true joy in life, the being used for a purpose recognized by yourself as a mighty one; the being a force of nature instead of a feverish, selfish little clod of ailments and grievances complaining that the world will not devote itself to making you happy.

I am of the opinion that my life belongs to the whole community, and as long as I live, it is my privilege to do for it whatever I can.

I want to be thoroughly used up when I die, for the harder I work the more I live. I rejoice in life for its own sake. Life is no "brief candle" for me. It is a sort of splendid torch which I have got hold of for the moment, and I want to make it burn as brightly as possible before handing it on to future generations.

Your torch can be your career in real estate, and I hope you make your torch burn as brightly as possible. I hope to see you at one of my seminars and that you come up to me and tell me you're making a six-figure income and you have everything you want in your life.

Keep in mind that in this profession we don't just help people buy and sell real estate, we actually help them to get to their next level. The more people who you touch and help get to their next level, the more money you are going to make. The money you make is a reflection of how many people you have helped. So go out there and help a lot of people.

I wish you the best—have a Powerful Career!

Index

A

AAA (American Automobile
    Association) membership, 68
Absentee owners, prospecting,
    135–137
Administrative support, 52
Advantage, FEA listing conversation,
    157–158
Advertising and promotion
    and company choice, 46, 54–55
    expenses, 21–23, 40
    farming, 141–142
    fonts, in advertising copy, 145–146
    mailing, 22–23, 69, 113–115,
        141, 171
    premiums for, 23
    prospecting, 85–86, 144–146
    public open house, 129–132
Advice
    listing conversation, 148, 149,
        152–162
    from other agents, 10–11
Aggressiveness
    "hard" approach to FSBOs, 102–109
    of successful agent, 7–8
American Automobile Association
    (AAA) membership, 68
Analytical skills, commercial real
    estate, 16–17
Answering machines, FSBOs, 116
Appearance and clothing, 67
Appointments, FSBOs, 100, 104, 106
    (*See also* Listing conversations)
Appraisers, and sold data, 162
Aroma, in open house, 131

Attitude, 2, 9–11
Automobile expenses, 21, 23, 67, 222
Average commission per sale, 26–28

B

Bank appraisers, and sold data, 162
Best time to call FSBOs, 115–116
Book for listing conversation,
    153–155
Brokers and broker-managers,
    40, 42–43, 45–47
    (*See also* Real estate companies)
Buffett, Warren, 8
Builders, prospecting, 137–139
Business cards, prospecting, 143–144
Business expenses, starting your
    career, 20–22, 24–25
Business owner mentality, 9
Buyer-agency agreement, 13
Buyers
    categorizing, 166
    commission splits, 26–27, 40
    filing system for, 70–71, 73
    generating, for listings, 168–170
    playing with, 165–170
    Real Estate Buddy, 59
    showing properties to, 166–168
    and successful agents, 13–14
    supplies in car for, 68–69
    time required by, 12

C

Calculating expenses, 24–25
"Calling around" new listings, 126–127

Calls (*See* Knocking on doors;
Telephone calls)
Cameras, 22, 66
CAP (confidence, aggressiveness,
persistence), 6–9
Car expenses, 21, 22, 23, 67
Categorizing buyers, 166
Characteristics of successful agents
(*See* Successful agent characteristics)
Clients, orphan, 121–126
(*See also* Buyers; Sellers)
Clothing and appearance, 67
Code of Ethics, NAR, 153
Cold calling and farming, 140–143
College, saving for kid's, 65
Color laser printers, 22, 66
Commercial real estate, 15–18
Commissions
average per sale, 26–28
buyer/seller splits, 26–27, 40
commercial real estate, 15–16
company splits, 47–48
100 percent commission model,
39–41, 48
Real Estate Buddy Program,
59–61, 63
savings needed to start your
career, 24–25
Commitment
homeowner goals, and prospecting,
103–105, 119–120
by successful agents, 1–4
Community group, prospecting,
139–140
Community study call, 128–129
Companies (*See* Real estate
companies)
Compensation (*See* Commissions)
Competition, commercial
real estate, 16
Computers, 21, 66
Confidence of successful agents, 6–7
Contacts, 66, 96–97
(*See also* Prospecting for listings)
Contract folders, 70
Conversations, listing (*See* Listing
conversations)
Cover letter for mailings, 114

Covey, Steven, 5
Credentials, listing conversation
book, 153–154, 156

D

Daily to-do list, 34
Database, prospecting, 96–97
Developers, prospecting, 137–139
Dictor, Ann, 69–70
Digital cameras, 22, 66
Digital vs. paper filing system, 73–74
Director technique, 109–110
Discount brokerage companies, 39
Doors (*See* Knocking on doors)

E

E–mail, 76
E–Myth Revisited (Gerber), 64
Education and training
about builders, 138–139
expenses, 21
for real estate license, 37
promotions and prospecting,
85–86
real estate companies, 43–44
research, first 90 days of success,
172–173
of successful agents, 3–4
Engagement, listing conversation,
148, 150–152
Environment of company
office, 45–46
E&O (Errors and Omission)
insurance, 21
Equipment, organization of, 66–69
Errors and Omission (E&O)
insurance, 21
Expenses
business expenses, 20–22, 24–25
calculating, 24–25
car, 21, 22, 23, 67
E&O insurance, 21
optional, 22–23
organization and management, 65
personal expenses, 19–20, 24–25
prospecting, 85–86
starting your career, 19–25

taxes, 25–26
(*See also* Advertising and
promotion)
Expired listings, 72–73, 117–121
Explanation, FEA listing conversation,
157–158

F

Failure and persistence, 8
Family considerations, starting
career, 29–33
Farming, 140–143
FEA (feature, explain, advantage)
listing conversation, 157–158
Fear, and first 90 days of success, 174
Feature, FEA listing conversation,
157–158
Filing system, 69–75
digital vs. paper, 73–74
for buyers, 73
for clients, 70–71
for leads, 71–73
for sellers, 70–73
for the market, 69–70
organization, 69–75
Finding FSBOs, 101
First 90 days, 171–175
Floor time, 51
Follow-up
first 90 days of success, 172
FSBOs, 112–115
Fonts, in advertising copy, 145–146
For Sale By Owner (FSBO), 99–116
as best leads, 90
best time to call, 115–116
building relationships with, 86–88
finding, 101
follow-up, 112–115
FSBO File Box, 71–72
gathering information, 104–105
getting appointment, 100,
104, 106
getting listing, 100
"hard" approach to, 102–109
invite action, 106–109
knocking on doors, 111–112
leaving a message, 116

mailings, 113–115
percentage that end up with
agent, 90
prospecting, 134–135
"soft" approach to, 109–110
telephone calls to, 100, 102–110,
115–116
thank-you notes, 112–113
Franchise companies, 38–41, 43–44
FSBO (*See* For Sale By Owner [FSBO])
Full vs. part-time work, 28–29

G

Gathering information, FSBOs,
104–105
Generating buyers, for listings,
168–170
Gerber, Michael, 64
Goal setting, 30–31, 53
Google, 76
Graduated split/split rollback, 48

H

Handling objections, listing
conversation, 164–165
"Hard" approach to FSBOs, 102–109
Harney, Steve, 10
Hopkins, Tom, 113
House tours
listing conversation, 149–150
notebook, for marketing notes,
69–70
open houses, 129–134

I

"I Have Buyers" call, 127–128
Impression, interview, 49–50
In Search of Excellence (Peters), 9–10
Influence, sphere of, 94–97, 171–172
Insurance, E&O, 21
Internet service, 76
Interviews
listing conversations, 147–170
questions to ask companies,
42–43, 52–55
Real Estate Buddy, 62–63
Investment, real estate as, 18, 53–54

Invitation, neighborhood open
  house, 132–134
Inviting action, prospecting,
  106–109, 120–121

J

"Just Sold" call, 128

K

Knocking on doors
  farming, 142–143
  FSBOs, 111–112
  "I Have Buyers" call, 127–128
  "Just Sold" call, 128
  new listing "calling around,"
    126–127
Knowledge, commercial real
  estate, 16–17

L

Laptop computers, 21, 66
Large independent companies, 38
Leads
  building relationships with, 87–88
  company management of, 47
  filing system for, 71–73
  (*See also* Prospecting for listings)
Leaving a message, FSBOs, 116
Letters (*See* Notes and letters)
License, real estate, 37
License, to sell real estate, 37
The List (*See* Multiple Listing
  Service [MLS])
Listing(s)
  as added value to homeowner, 93
  commission, 26–27, 40
  company call handling, 55
  dot board, 74–75
  expired, 72–73, 117–121
  filing system for sellers, 70–73
  MLS listings this year vs. last year, 77
  prospecting, 81–83, 93–94
  Real Estate Buddy, 57–63
  success and working with
    sellers, 13–14
  (*See also* Prospecting for listings)

Listing agreements, 162–164
Listing conversations, 147–170
  advising, 148, 149, 152–162
  book for, 153–155
  conversation vs. presentation
    terms, 147–148
  engagement, 148, 150–152
  FEA tool, 157–158
  handling objections, 164–165
  listing agreement, 162–164
  playing with buyers, 165–170
  price, 151–152, 160–162
  rapport building, 148, 149–150
  REAL process, 148–149
Location of company office, 44–45

M

Magnets for car, 22
Mailings, 22–23, 69, 113–115,
  141, 171
Maps, 68
The market, filing system for, 69–70
Market share of companies, 42–43
Marketing plan, in listing
  conversation book, 154–155, 156
Mentoring program, 53, 56–63
MLS (*See* Multiple Listing Service
  [MLS])
Mom-and-pop companies, 37–38
Money (*See* Commissions)
Motivation, first 90 days of success, 173
Multiple Listing Service (MLS)
  dues, 20
  expired listings, 72–73, 117–118
  FEA tool, 157–158
  National Association of Realtors
    (NAR), 20, 35–36, 153
  research, first 90 days of success, 172
  technical uses for, 77–79
Multiple Listing Service (MLS)
  statistics
  average days on market, 78
  listings this year vs. last year, 77
  market saturation rate (MSR),
    78–79
  number of sales this year vs. last
    year, 78

sales price this year vs. last year, 78, 160–161

N

National Association of Realtors (NAR), 20, 35–36, 153
(*See also* Multiple Listing Service [MLS])
Neighborhood open house, 132–134
New listing "calling around," 126–127
Nietzsche, Frederich, 8
Notebook, for marketing, 69–70
Notes and letters
first 90 days of success, 172
to office "orphans," 122
sphere of influence, 95–96
thank-you notes, 68, 112–113

O

Objections, listing conversation, 164–165
Office (*See* Real estate companies)
Office supplies, 222
Old FSBOs, 134–135
100 percent commission model, 39–41, 48
Open houses, 129–134
Optional expenses, starting your career, 22–23
Organization, 64–79
equipment and supplies, 66–69
filing system, 69–75
importance of, 64–65
listing dot board, 74–75
money and expense management, 65
technology as tool, 75–79
Orphan clients, 121–126
Ownership of real estate companies, 36

P

Palm Pilot, 22, 67
Paper vs. digital filing system, 73–74
Part vs. full-time work, 28–29
Passion and prospecting, 86
Persistence, 8–9

Personal considerations, starting your career, 28–29
Personal expenses, starting your career, 19–20, 24–25
Peters, Tom, 9–10
Photograph of agent, 66–67
Playing with buyers, listing conversation, 165–170
PMI (private mortgage insurance), 123–124
Policies and procedures manual, 50
Positive attitude, 2, 9–11
Pre-listing conversation, neighborhood open house, 132–134
Presentation (*See* Listing conversations)
Price
filing buyers by range of, 73
listing conversation, 151–152, 160–162
Printers, 22, 66
Private mortgage insurance (PMI), 123–124
Problem solving attitude, 9–11
Professionalism, commercial real estate, 15
Promotion (*See* Advertising and promotion)
Prospecting for listings, 80–146
absentee owners, 135–137
adding value to homeowners, 93
advertising and promotion, 85–86, 144–146
aggressiveness, 7–8
approaches and concepts, 83–94
builders, 137–139
calling around new listings, 126–127
community groups, 139–140
community study call, 128–129
contact database, 96–97
don't worry about next step, 91–92
every homeowner as lead, 88–90
expired listings, 72–73, 117–121
farming, 140–143
as first link to success, 84–85

with FSBOs, 99–116, 134–135
"I have buyers" call, 127–128
importance of, 80–81
"Just Sold" call, 128
listings as promotion, 94
mastering, 97–98
open house, 129–134
orphan clients, 121–126
passion, 86
relationship building, 86–88
schedule creation, 92–93, 97–98
special business cards, 143–144
sphere of influence, 94–97
techniques for, 11–12, 94–98
thank-you notes, 68
time required, 11
updated market analysis, 88–90,
    96, 125–126
vacant land, 137–139
(*See also* Leads)
Public open house, 129–132

R

Rapport, listing conversation,
    148, 149–150
Real estate agents
    average income of, 55
    licensing, 37
    mix in office, 52–53
    National Association of Realtors
        (NAR), 20, 35–36, 153
    as Real Estate Buddy, 57–63
    (*See also* Successful agent
        characteristics; *specific topics*)
Real Estate Buddy Program, 56–63
Real estate companies, 35–48
    choice considerations, 41–48
    commission splits, 47–48
    comparison between, and
        interview, 50
    discount brokerage, 39
    first 90 days of success, 173
    franchises, 38–41
    interviewing with, 42–43, 52–55
    large independent companies, 38
    lead management, 47
    in listing conversation book, 154
    market share, 42–43

mom-and-pop, 37–38
National Association of Realtors
    (NAR), 20, 35–36, 153
office environment, 45–46
office location, 44–45
100 percent model, 39–41, 48
ownership, 36
policies and procedures manual, 50
promotion, 46
real estate license, 37
training, 43–44
types of, 37–41
REAL process, listing, 148–149
Realtor, 35
Realtor-Associate, 36
Rejection and persistence, 8
Relationship building, prospecting,
    86–88
Retirement, savings for, 65
Reverse lookup, 71–72

S

Savings, needed to start your career,
    24–25
Scheduling and time management
    commercial real estate, 16
    daily to-do list, 34
    family time, 31–32
    prospecting, 92–93, 97–98
    by successful agents, 11–13
Sellers
    filing system for, 70–73
    working with, 13–14
    (*See also* Listing[s])
Seven Habits of Highly Effective People
    (Covey), 5
Shaw, George Bernard, 174
Showing properties to buyers,
    166–168
Signs, public open house, 130–131
Smell, in open house, 131
"Soft" approach to FSBOs, 109–110
Sold prices, 78, 160–161
Spare tire, 69
Special business cards, 143–144
Sphere of influence, 94–97, 171–172
"A Splendid Torch" (Shaw), 174
Starting your career, 19–34

average commission per sale, 26–28
daily to-do list, 34
expenses, 19–25
family considerations, 29–33
personal considerations, 28–29
savings needed, 24–25
taxes, 25–26
Stationery, 67, 68
Successful agent characteristics, 1–18
aggressiveness, 7–8
attitude, 2
business owner mentality, 9
buyer focus, 13–14
CAP, 6–9
commercial real estate, 15–18
commitment, 1–4
confidence, 6–7
education and training, 3–4
first 90 days, 171–175
investing in real estate, 18
persistence, 8–9
positive attitude, 2
problem solving attitude, 9–11
seller focus, 13–14
time management, 11–13
vision, 4–6
Supplies, organization of, 66–69
S.U.R.E Results™ seminars, 176

T

Tape measure, 66
Tape recorder, 68
Taxes, 25–26
Technology
in company, 53
computers, 21, 66

digital cameras, 22, 66
e-mail, 76
expenses for, 21–22
filing and organization, 73–79
Web sites, 22, 51, 101
Telephone calls
community study call, 128–129
farming, 142–143
to FSBOs, 100, 102–110, 115–116
"I Have Buyers" call, 127–128
"Just Sold" call, 128
10-10-20 Rule, 126
Thank–you notes, 68, 112–113
Time management (*See* Scheduling
and time management)
To-do list, daily, 34
Training (*See* Education and
training)

U

Updated market analysis, 88–90, 96,
125–126
Upromise.com, 65

V

Vacant land, prospecting,
137–139
Vision Board, 6
Vision of successful agents, 4–6
Visual reference, listing conversation
book, 152–155

W

Wasmeier, Markus, 92
Web sites, 22, 51, 101

About the Author

Since 1990, Darryl Davis has been traveling around the world, coaching agents and brokers on how to achieve their next level of success. In 1993, he created The POWER Program, a yearlong training and coaching program whereby agents who complete the program, on the average, double their production over their previous year. In addition, he is the creator of the nationally acclaimed three-day training course called S.U.R.E. Results™ (Success is Unlimited in Real Estate), the only program of its kind that guarantees that agents will earn while they learn!

Darryl's training and speaking experience cover a wide variety of successful ventures. He has been a top-rated speaker at the NAR convention since 1999. In every venue—from local board functions to the National Association of Realtors® convention—Darryl's contagious enthusiasm, hilarious humor, flawless delivery, and impeccable integrity make for dynamic presentations of real-world skills, techniques, and dialogues designed to increase the production and effectiveness of all the sales professionals who attend them.

But Darryl is much more than a speaker. He is also an entertainer, having been spotlighted at Caroline's Comedy Club sharing the same stage as Dave Chappelle, Chris Rock, Jay Leno, Rosie O'Donnell, Rita Rudner, Jerry Seinfeld, and others. He is also listed in *Who's Who Worldwide*.

Darryl's innovation, creativity, and masterful approach have made his seminars highly requested throughout the real estate industry. Like his ecstatic clients and his successful students, you too will be delighted with what Darryl shares in this book.

Find out more at www.DarrylDavisSeminars.com or www. NewAgent Success.com or call our office toll-free at (800) 395-3905.